Latin American Inflation

LATIN AMERICAN INFLATION

Theoretical Interpretations
and
Empirical Results

JULIO HAROLD COLE

PRAEGER

New York
Westport, Connecticut
London

Library of Congress Cataloging-in-Publication Data

Cole, Julio Harold.

    Latin American inflation.

    Bibliography: p.
    Includes index.
    1. Latin America—Economic conditions—1945-   .
2. Inflation (Finance)—Latin America. 3. Bolivia—
Economic conditions—1982-   . 4. Inflation
(Finance)—Bolivia. I. Title.
HC125.C62 1987   332.4'1'098   87-15156
ISBN 0-275-92809-8 (alk. paper)

Library of Congress Catalog Card Number: 87-15156
ISBN: 0-275-92809-8

First published in 1987

Praeger Publishers, One Madison Avenue, New York, NY 10010
A division of Greenwood Press, Inc.

Printed in the United States of America

∞

The paper used in this book complies with the Permanent Paper Standard
issued by the National Information Standards Organization (Z39.48-1984).

10 9 8 7 6 5 4 3 2 1

Para Gina y Joecito,

Con todo mi amor,

And for Musso Ayau and Joe Keck,

I have finished my course,
I have kept the faith.

2 Tim. 4:7

There cannot, in short, be intrinsically a more insignificant thing, in the economy of society, than money; except in the character of a contrivance for sparing time and labor. It is a machine for doing quickly and commodiously, what could be done, though less quickly and commodiously, without it; and like many other kinds of machinery, it only exerts a distinct and independent influence of its own when it gets out of order.

—John Stuart Mill, *Principles of Political Economy*

Irredeemable paper money has almost invariably proved a curse to the country employing it.

—Irving Fisher, *The Purchasing Power of Money*

CONTENTS

Preface   xi

Acknowledgments   xv

1. INFLATION IN LATIN AMERICA:
        A MONETARIST VIEW   1

2. AN ALTERNATIVE VIEW: THE STRUCTURALIST
        ARGUMENT REVISITED   25

3. INFLATION IN A SMALL COUNTRY: A CASE
        STUDY OF BOLIVIA   39

4. A SUMMING UP   65

Appendix—STATISTICAL ASPECTS OF INFLATION RATES   71

Bibliography   81

Index   87

About the Author   91

PREFACE

This book aims to provide in four largely self-contained sections an interpretation of Latin American inflation from the point of view of an applied statistician. Though some of the more technical discussions may not be strictly essential for following the general line of argument, much of the book does assume some prior knowledge of mathematics and statistics, and it does not, on the other hand, seek to impart such knowledge. Large sections of the book are thus not likely to be easy reading, and there is an obligation therefore to keep it short.

Though the separate sections may seem at first glance not only self-contained, but even somewhat unrelated to each other, the book nonetheless has a unifying theme, and since it is a short book I hope that the theme will become clear to the reader. The book is compressed enough as it is, but it might be useful in a Preface to summarize the argument a bit further. At a purely formal level a simple "monetarist" theory can explain Latin American inflation, though it cannot by itself provide an explanation in terms of the "ultimate causes" of monetary growth cum price inflation. This is the basis of the structuralist critique, which attempts to provide an explanation in this deeper sense. The structuralist theses, however, do not stand up to rigorous empirical testing. The moral of the story is that, while a monetarist framework must underlie any explanation of inflation, the diversity of observed experiences rules out any general theory in the deeper sense, and specific inflationary episodes must perforce be explained in terms of country-specific circumstances. The Bolivian experience is a case in point. The historical approach, moreover, highlights the human element, which tends to be disregarded in formal monetarist-type analyses, as well as in general theories such as structuralism. (A distorted perspective is perhaps an unavoidable by-product of a statistical approach to the study of social phenomena, as events tend to be viewed as if from the wrong end of a telescope—the figures look small, and happenings often appear correspondingly trivial.)

Chapter 1 is devoted to a statistical analysis of the long-run inflation rates of 16 Latin American countries. I am aware, of course, that statistical analysis per se is practically worthless without a prior theoretical framework, since statistical hypothesis testing is merely a procedure for choosing between two or more specified alternatives, and its outcome in any particular instance depends not only upon the criteria on the basis of which the choice is to be made, but particularly upon the nature of the admissible alternatives. Since the determination of a set of all possible alternatives lies beyond the scope of the test procedure itself, no analysis of real phenomena can possibly be reduced to an automatic sequence of statistical tests. A preliminary section deals, therefore, with the theoretical framework for the analysis, discusses the Quantity Theory of Money as a theory of the demand for money, and derives the basic regression equation which will be applied to the Latin American data. My interpretation of the quantity theory has been much influenced by the work of Prof. Milton Friedman (1956, 1968, 1969), though of course he might not endorse the particular interpretation that I have applied throughout. The theoretical discussion is then followed by an empirical analysis of the Latin American data for the period 1970–80. The results are then compared with data for the same group of countries for an earlier period (1950–69), and with more recent data for the early 1980s. The final section deals with the sources of monetary growth in Latin America, and draws some conclusions regarding the correlation-causation issue.

No strictly monetarist analysis of inflation can claim much by way of originality. In fact, one of my main objectives is to show that pervasive inflation in Latin America does not require any "new" or "own" theory, since it can be fully explained in terms of well-established theoretical categories. Restatement of old truths does serve a useful purpose, however, though perhaps not one calling in itself for a major ovation.

As I have mentioned above in passing, the empirical analysis of Chapter 1 is in terms of long-run inflation rates, or, more precisely, in terms of average annual inflation rates over relatively long periods. This is partly due to convenience in reducing to manageable proportions an otherwise unwieldy mass of data, though I believe that there are also methodological grounds for justifying such a preference. Specifically, I am convinced that there is virtually no information to be derived from the analysis of short-run inflation rates, since the behavior of inflation in the short run exhibits a pattern that is practically identical to that of a random walk. (The Appendix is devoted to this and related topics.)

The main alternative to the monetarist analysis, the structuralist theory of Latin American inflation, is discussed at length in Chapter 2. A preliminary section summarizes the structuralist literature, and states its principal empirical implications. These are then subjected to empirical tests. Since it will become apparent in the course of the discussion, I might as well state from the outset that I do not sympathize with the structuralist view, though I have tried my utmost to provide a fair and unbiased presentation. In this I may not have been wholly successful, but I am sure that an independent scrutiny of the writings of major structuralist authors will confirm that I have summarized that literature responsibly and with care.

Chapter 3 is an analysis of the recent Bolivian hyperinflation. Background sections discuss economic and political developments culminating in the debacle of 1982. The events of that year are then discussed in detail. The ensuing hyperinflation is described, stressing the human as well as the political and economic aspects. Successive stabilization efforts are discussed, particularly the program of August 1985, which finally ended the inflation.

Apart from standard statistical, historical, and journalistic sources, my discussion draws heavily upon my own personal experience in Bolivia during most of the period under review, which perhaps explains the sometimes bitter tone that more than one commentator has pointed out to me. On rereading this chapter I have also become aware that the discussion by the nature of its subject does injustice to the Bolivian people. Because it concentrates upon a low point in Bolivia's history, the negative aspects predominate. The likeableness, the artistic vein and philosophic cast of mind, the strength of character, innate dignity and self-respect, intelligence and quickness of mind, good humor, stamina and capacity for work of the average Bolivian have not come through in proper proportion. I can only acknowledge this with regret.

Though I hold no similar regard for Bolivia's rulers, I must admit that here too I may have been guilty of some injustice. To be sure, too many Bolivian politicians have been constitutionally averse to influencing events, holders with no goal but to hold, when they have not been outright conscienceless, unprincipled crooks, doing their damage while strutting their brief seasons. Sweeping condemnations come easily in retrospect, however, as the historian often overlooks the fact that statesmen, even when they are men of utter integrity and high performance with a complete grasp of the situation, must make their decisions in contemporary context without the benefit of hindsight. Crises work themselves out in stages without history's vantage point in seeing the whole event as well as its aftermath. On the other hand, there was nothing inevitable about the Bolivian crisis, which might well have unfolded otherwise, for in the course of the process there were many likely alternatives that could have been chosen, might-have-beens only barely missed. This is the hardest thing to imagine in looking at the past, since what happened seems to be, after all, only what had to happen—there are no dice in heaven. The most impressive contrary evidence, however, is the simple fact that no one knows beforehand how a story will end.

I would like to express my gratitude to Mr. Michael Fisher, formerly of Praeger Publishers, for encouragement in the initial stages of the undertaking. Special debts of thanks are due to Dr. Michel R. Vetsuypens, my old classmate from Rochester, now of SMU in Dallas, Texas, upon whom I have inflicted countless versions of my work over the past few years, and whose scathing comments have always been helpful (if not always welcome!), and to Sr. J. Roberto Brenes, my favorite colleague, who has always expressed interest in my researches, even though I don't agree in the least with his views on methodology. Thanks are also due to Sr. Luis Palomo G., Marroquín Computing Center, for able programming assistance. I cannot close without acknowledging the help of my wife, who through thick and thin has unfailingly provided support above and beyond the call of duty. Naturally, I assume full responsibility for any errors of fact, interpretation, or translation.

J. H. C.

ACKNOWLEDGMENTS

Chapter 1 includes material that was first published in the article "Inflation in Latin America, 1970–80," *Environment and Planning C: Government and Policy*, vol. 4 (February 1986), pp. 31–41, and is reproduced by permission of Pion, Ltd., London. Chapter 3 includes material published originally in the article "Inflación en un País Pequeño: El Caso de Bolivia," *Revista Occidental*, Año 2, Nos. 2-3 (1985), pp. 167–88, which is reproduced by permission of the publishers.

Latin American
Inflation

CHAPTER 1

INFLATION IN LATIN AMERICA:
A MONETARIST VIEW

Inflation is not a new phenomenon in Latin America. Indeed, it is often stated that in this region inflation is a way of life, the natural state of affairs. To be sure, there are quite a few cases where this generalization is not completely accurate, and in some cases it is decidedly unfair, though it does describe concisely the monetary history of many Latin American countries.

From a strictly economic point of view, however, there is nothing very special about the Latin American inflations. Ultimately, no doubt, these inflations have their origins in very peculiar historico-political circumstances, concerning which the economist as such cannot shed much light. This is the task of historians and political scientists. On the other hand, the experience of decades of chronic inflation cannot help but produce some interesting sociocultural types, which deserve the attention of sociologists and social psychologists. But if we abstract from these political factors, and from the social implications, the fact is that the Latin American inflations are not very different from the inflations that have occurred in other regions and periods.

This is not meant to slight the enormous magnitude of the inflations that have taken place in some Latin American countries. Indeed, this is the first thing that strikes the eye when one examines the available data. At the end of 1980, for instance, consumer prices in Chile were 4,365 times higher than at the end of 1970, in Argentina 2,830 times higher, and 136 times higher in Uruguay. Compare with inflation in the United States, where prices "only" doubled over the same decade. More recently, inflation in Bolivia up to mid-1985 has established a relative postwar world's record (the case of Bolivia is treated in detail in Chapter 3). These extreme inflations certainly require an explanation.

On the other hand, the data also show that galloping inflation does not characterize all of Latin America. In fact, the inflationary experience of these countries has been diverse—eight countries, for instance, had average rates of inflation which were less than 15% per annum during the decade 1970-80 (see Table 1.1). This also calls for explanation.

According to an old and reputable tradition in monetary economics, inflation is essentially a monetary problem—significant changes in the price level are due to changes in the amount of money in circulation. Furthermore, the magnitude of inflation depends upon the magnitude of the increase in the money supply, implying that countries with high rates of monetary growth will also have high rates of inflation, and that low inflation countries will exhibit correspondingly lower rates of monetary growth. There is a considerable volume of empirical evidence in favor of this hypothesis, which is known as the Quantity Theory of Money, and it is not surprising, then, that the Latin American experience also confirms the hypothesis. The Latin American data are particularly interesting from a statistical point of view, because the inflationary experience of these countries has been highly varied, which allows to determine the effect of monetary growth with a high degree of precision. Prior to a detailed analysis of the data, however, a previous examination of the theoretical framework for the analysis is in order.

THEORETICAL FRAMEWORK

The Quantity Theory of Money is first and foremost a theory of the demand for money. At the core of this theory lies a fundamental conceptual distinction between the *nominal* quantity of money, which can be usefully referred to as the money supply, and the *real* quantity of money, which is the money supply expressed in terms of its purchasing power. The demand for money is best regarded as a real rather than a nominal magnitude, and may be defined as the amount of real purchasing power that the public desires to hold in the form of money, or, alternatively, as the fraction of real income that the public desires to hold in money form rather than spend immediately on goods and services or invest in income-yielding nonmoney assets.

The central proposition of the quantity theory is that there is a definite real quantity of money that a given community will desire to hold under any given set of circumstances, and that this desired real quantity of money (demand for money) will not generally change as a result of a change in the (nominal) money supply. Therefore, demand will not always necessarily equal supply, since the nominal quantity of money actually held might correspond, at current prices, to a real quantity in excess of that which is desired. If so, individuals will then seek to reduce their excess money balances by increasing their monetary outlays. However, as Friedman points out, "one man's expenditures are another man's receipts. One man can reduce his nominal money balances only by persuading someone else to increase his. The community as a whole cannot in general spend more than it receives" (1968, p. 434). Nonetheless, a communitywide attempt to do so will have predictable consequences. In effect,

> If prices and income are free to change, the attempt to spend more will raise the nominal volume of expenditures and receipts, which will lead to a bidding up of prices and perhaps also to an increase in output. If prices are fixed by custom or by government edict, the attempt to spend more either will be matched by an increase in goods or services or will produce "shortages" and "queues." These in turn will raise the effective prices and are likely sooner or later to force changes in official prices. The initial excess of money balances will therefore tend to be eliminated, . . . by either a reduction in the real quantity held through price rises or an increase in the real quantity desired through output increases (Friedman, 1968, p. 434).

This central distinction between the demand for real money balances and the nominal supply of money does not imply that the demand for money is constant, though all variants of the quantity theory hold that changes in the demand for money tend to proceed slowly and gradually, and in general independently of changes in the money supply, which in contrast can and frequently does change substantially and independently of any changes in the demand for money.

Determinants of the Demand for Money

That long-run changes in the demand for money are determined mainly by changes in real income is suggested by a well-established empirical fact, namely, the relative stability of the ratio of the nominal money supply to nominal income. Since this ratio amounts to the same thing as the ratio of the real money supply to real income, the stability of this ratio even in the face of substantial changes in nominal incomes and price levels implies that the demand for real money balances is in some way functionally related to the level of real income. The empirical evidence in this regard is so abundant that it would be idle to exhaustively cite a list of relevant references. Suffice it to note that the phenomenon is so pervasive that a substantial and rapid rise in the measured money/income ratio in any given country is more likely presumptive evidence of an underestimation of measured nominal income than of an actual increase in the demand for money.[1]

The empirical nature of this fact is best illustrated by the lack of any convincing theoretical explanation of why this is so, much less why it *should* be so, nor are there strictly theoretical reasons for believing that the income-elasticity of demand for money should be either less than unitary (income-inelastic), greater than unitary (income-elastic), or strictly unitary.[2] Of course, the fact in question can always be "explained" by postulating a constant "income-elasticity of demand for money," though statements of this kind are at best a summary description of empirical observations, if not a roundabout admission of ignorance. It is a fact nonetheless, and it moreover goes far toward providing a theoretical explanation of the phenomenon of price inflation.

In the literature on the demand for money, the opportunity cost of holding money balances is often identified as another major factor affecting money demand. In this literature, money in its store of value-role is viewed as a form of wealth, and the demand for cash balances as a form of holding wealth. The factors that determine the distribution of wealth into money and nonmonies are then seen as the relevant arguments in the money demand function. In this approach the attractiveness of alternative forms of holding wealth, relative to the services yielded by money itself, should therefore have an important impact on the desired level of money balances. Alternatively, at the margin the demand for money should depend upon the opportunity cost of holding wealth in money form rather than in income-yielding liquid assets. The cost of holding money is of course interpreted broadly so as to include expected real losses due to changes in the purchasing power of the monetary unit.

To be sure, price-theoretic considerations (as well as simple common sense) dictate that the cost of holding money *should* affect the demand for real cash balances, but the question as to the extent of the cost-elasticity of money demand, and whether the actual variability of the relevant cost variable is such as to induce significant variability in money demand, is an empirical one. In this regard, the early theoretical literature on the effect of interest rates on money demand, and the magnitude of the implied elasticities, stands in striking contrast to the empirical results obtained.

In early formulations in the Keynesian tradition, for instance, the demand for money was viewed as highly interest-elastic at low levels of interest rates, the so-called "liquidity trap," with a correspondingly unstable demand for money, changes in the money supply merely being offset by compensating changes in demand. The demand for money was thus a highly unstable and erratic "will o'the wisp," generally varying in the same direction as that of the nominal money supply. To be sure, Keynes himself regarded the liquidity trap as a limiting case (1936, p. 207), and subsequent research has yielded no evidence whatsoever that such conditions can prevail under remotely plausible circumstances, though most later theoretical literature continued to show a strong presumption in favor of a significant and sizeable interest-elasticity of money demand. Baumol's (1952) inventory-theoretic approach, for instance, posited conditions which yielded a theoretical elasticity of -0.5, as well as an income-elasticity of 0.5 (suggesting economies of scale in the use of cash balances with rising incomes).

Tobin's (1958) portfolio-theory approach provided additional theoretical grounds from a different viewpoint, while Gurley and Shaw (1960) emphasized the close substitutability between money, narrowly defined, and other types of financial assets, suggesting that cash holdings should be sensitive to changes in rates of return on alternative assets.

Given the strong theoretical rationale for an interest-sensitive money demand function, the surprising result of the host of empirical studies that have been made (mostly of U.S. data), is not that the interest rate is in fact a statistically significant variable, but rather the relatively small magnitude of the resulting estimates. The results are of course expected to vary across studies insofar as they apply a wide range of statistical estimation procedures to different definitions of the money supply, using different time periods and sets of explanatory variables, alternative functional forms, and data with different periodicities (annual, quarterly, cycle-averages). Some broad patterns emerge nonetheless. A consistent finding of the 13 studies surveyed by Boorman (1980) is that the demand for money balances is relatively interest-inelastic when the short-term interest rate is used, with estimates ranging from -0.07 to -0.2. (The estimates increase to over -0.5 only when long-run interest rates are used, although there seems to be fairly wide agreement that the short-term rate is a more relevant measure of the opportunity cost of holding money instead of its close substitutes.) A large number of studies, mostly based on quarterly data, relating money demand in the U.S. to returns on money substitutes, were surveyed by Feige and Pearce (1977) and again the reported empirical elasticities are quite small.

Though a great deal of research has been devoted to "The Search for a Stable Money Demand Function," to quote the title of a major review article (Judd and Scadding, 1982), it is worthwhile to recall that most of this empirical effort has been limited to the study of U.S. data, and particularly to the postwar experience of that country. The question naturally arises whether such results as have been obtained can be generalized from this relatively limited sample.

To date there is still a relative paucity of published empirical research on money demand outside the U.S. To be sure, Cagan's classic study of hyperinflations (Cagan, 1956), which in fact predated much of the available empirical work on money demand, showed that in contrast to the U.S. studies, money demand is highly sensitive to the opportunity cost of holding real monetary balances—indeed, under these conditions inflationary expectations swamp the effects of any other relevant variable. The question that remains, however, is whether the demand for money is cost-sensitive under less than hyperinflationary conditions. What little evidence there is tends to show that, if the cost variable is relevant at all, the cost-elasticity may be even smaller than the estimates obtained from the U.S. data.

In Harberger's (1963) regression study of Chilean inflation, the coefficient of an appropriately defined opportunity cost variable (the past change in the rate of inflation) was marginally significant with an absolute value of 0.2, which is consistent with the U.S. studies, although a subsequent study by Vogel (1974) extending Harberger's analysis to 16 Latin American countries yielded an average value of 0.07 in separate regressions (and coefficients with the "wrong" sign in five cases), and nonsignificant coefficients in pooled regressions. A characteristic of studies of money demand in developing countries is that they consistently fail to yield a significant cost-elasticity (a good example is the study by Crockett and Evans, 1980). In most of these studies the expected rate of inflation is regarded as the relevant cost variable, often proxied by past inflation rates.[3] To be sure, data problems are present in these studies to a much greater extent than in studies based on data for developed economies, though one may well wonder whether cost can be taken as significant if its effect cannot be detected.

A Minimal Monetarist Model of Inflation

As a first approximation, we may therefore adopt the working hypothesis that the demand for money depends exclusively upon the level of real income, and that, furthermore, the income-elasticity of money demand is constant. It can be readily shown that this implies a specific relation between the rate of inflation, the rate of growth in the nominal money supply, and the rate of growth of real income.

Adopting the notation defined in Note 2, this assumption may be stated formally as

$$e(M_r, Y_r) = \frac{\partial \ln\left(\dfrac{M}{P}\right)}{\partial \ln Y_r} = \alpha \qquad (1.1)$$

where α is a positive constant. Integrating and solving for $\ln P$ yields

$$\ln P = \ln M - \alpha \ln Y_r - C \qquad (1.2)$$

where C is a constant of integration. In particular, for any two given periods, t and o, we have

$$\ln P_t = \ln M_t - \alpha \ln Y_{rt} - C \qquad (1.2a)$$

and,

$$\ln P_o = \ln M_o - \alpha \ln Y_{ro} - C. \qquad (1.2b)$$

Subtracting (1.2b) from (1.2a), a property of logarithms yields

$$\ln\left(\frac{P_t}{P_o}\right) = \ln\left(\frac{M_t}{M_o}\right) - \alpha \ln\left(\frac{Y_{rt}}{Y_{ro}}\right) \tag{1.3}$$

or equivalently

$$\ln (1 + p) = \ln (1 + m) - \alpha \ln(1 + y_r) \tag{1.4}$$

where lower case letters denote the percentage change in the respective variables between periods o and t. This establishes the basic propositions usually associated with the quantity theory: a direct and positive relation between the (log-transformed) rate of monetary growth and the (log-transformed) rate of inflation, and a negative relation between the (log-transformed) rate of growth in real income and the (log-transformed) rate of inflation.

This equation, which is the basic working relationship that will be applied to the Latin American data in the following sections, derives directly from the assumption of a positive and constant income-elasticity of demand for money. (Mathematically, of course, equations (1.1) and (1.4) amount to the same thing, though (1.4) may seem more meaningful from the point of view of explaining variations in the rate of inflation.) To test the implied hypothesis, a linear regression of the following form can be estimated:

$$\ln (1 + p) = a_o + a_1 \ln (1 + m) + a_2 \ln (1 + y_r).$$

In terms of this regression equation, the version of the quantity theory expressed in (1.4) is equivalent to the following joint null hypothesis: $a_o = 0$, $a_1 = 1$, and $a_2 < 0$.

Again, it is well to recall that this simple relationship between p, m, and y_r derives from the basic simplifying assumption implied in (1.1), which deliberately ignores changes in the demand for money due to changes in the real cost of holding money balances, and specifically the effect of changes in inflationary expectations. For low to "moderate" values of m and p such effects may be empirically negligible, but it is clearly unrealistic to expect (1.4) to hold for any conceivable values, and it is well known from the study of hyperinflations that in conditions of extremely high values of m and p the rate of inflation tends to be much higher than the rate of monetary growth.

Bearing this caveat in mind, perhaps the most remarkable fact about the Latin American experience is that equation (1.4) provides a reasonably good fit to the data even at rates of inflation which could hardly be described as "moderate."

EMPIRICAL RESULTS

Table 1.1 shows the average annual rates of inflation, monetary growth, and real growth in 16 Latin American countries over the period 1970–80. Inflation was measured by means of two alternative price indexes: The Gross Domestic Product (GDP) deflator and the Consumer Price Index (CPI). The money supply is defined as the sum of currency outside banks plus demand deposits in banks, what is commonly referred to as M_1. Real growth is the rate of growth in real GDP. It is clearly seen that countries with high inflation also show high rates of monetary growth. With these data a regression analysis can be performed by estimating an equation of the following form:

$$\ln (1 + p) = a_o + a_1 \ln (1 + m) + a_2 \ln (1 + y_r)$$

where p, m, and y_r represent the average rates of change in the price index, the money supply, and real GDP, respectively. The data in Table 1.1 present several advantages for a statistical test of the quantity theory:

1. The expression of the data as ten-year average growth rates tends to minimize the error in estimates of average real growth, which is the variable with greatest measurement error. Thus, the measurement error of y_r relative to that of m is reduced (as measurement errors in m even in annual data are quite small). A better definition of y_r would have been the rate of change in real national income. However, data are not available, and the differences in rates of growth of real GDP and of real income are probably smaller than the actual sampling errors of measurement. Thus, no great improvement would probably result from refining the income measure.

2. The effect of price controls on measured inflation, potentially large in annual data, can be expected to "wash out" over a decade, and therefore total increase and average annual increase will not be much affected by this source of bias.

3. The effects of lags in the short-run effect of m can also be expected to work themselves out over a decade, and their effect on ten-year averages should be minor.

Therefore, for purposes of testing the quantity theory free from these disturbing factors, the data set in Table 1.1 is about as clean as can be achieved in practice, and, as noted above, the range of variation in inflationary experience is wide enough to permit the determination of monetary effects with a high degree of precision. Disturbances may arise because of

Table 1.1
Inflation, Monetary Growth, and Real Growth in Latin America, 1970–80
(average annual rates of change)

	Inflation		Monetary	Real
	GDP Deflator	CPI	Growth	Growth
Chile	147.1	131.2	145.3	2.4
Argentina	119.0	121.4	114.2	2.2
Uruguay	60.7	63.5	60.0	3.5
Brazil	40.3	38.1	44.2	8.4
Peru	31.3	32.5	33.1	3.0
Bolivia	20.9	19.7	25.4	4.8
Colombia	21.4	22.1	25.2	5.9
Mexico	17.6	17.5	24.4	5.2
Costa Rica	13.9	11.3	21.9	5.8
Ecuador	13.6	12.6	24.5	8.8
Venezuela	12.5	9.1	22.2	5.0
Paraguay	12.4	13.1	23.9	8.6
El Salvador	9.7	11.5	17.1	4.1
Guatemala	9.1	10.1	15.8	5.7
Dominican Republic	8.6	10.7	12.9	6.6
Honduras	8.0	8.4	14.4	3.6

Sources: *Inflation*. GDP Deflator: Computed from data reported in *Statistical Yearbook for Latin America and the Caribbean*, 1985 Edition (Santiago, Chile: United Nations, 1986); CPI: Computed from year-end data reported in *International Financial Statistics*, "Supplement on Price Statistics," Supplement Series No. 2, 1981.

Monetary Growth. Computed from data reported in *International Financial Statistics*, Dec 1977, Dec 1982, and Yearbook 1984.

Real Growth. Rates of growth in real GDP as reported in *World Development Report 1982* (Washington: World Bank, 1982).

the residual effect of these factors, and the effects of minor omitted variables. However, the statistical precautions should ensure that this residual effect is minimal, and if the quantity theory is true then omitted variables should have only a minor effect. Thus, the regression should have high explanatory power.

A source of bias may be the assumption of a_2 being the same for each country, which is not required, in a strict sense, by the model derived in the previous section of this chapter. However, the probable range of variation in a_2 is not great enough to ensure a large bias, since the range of variation in real growth rates is not great. The functional form of the regression postulates a linear relation between log-transformed rates of change. The use of this form, instead of a "straight" regression of the original data in Table 1.1, is because of the simple mathematical fact that the combined effect of separate rates of change is not additive, but rather the interaction of rates of change is multiplicative. Thus, the regression of untransformed variables can introduce bias due to omission of the interaction effect. (It may seem that this point is overbelabored, though it should be mentioned that this kind of oversight is not uncommon in empirical work—see, for example, Meiselman, 1975).

Using the two alternative measures of inflation and applying ordinary least squares we obtain the following estimates (standard deviations are given in parentheses):

Deflator: $\ln(1 + p) = -3.72 + 1.09 \ln(1 + m) -0.66 \ln(1 + y_r)$
$$(2.23) \quad (0.03) \qquad\qquad (0.32)$$
$$r^2 = 0.993$$

CPI: $\ln(1 + p) = -0.98 + 1.03 \ln(1 + m) -0.92 \ln(1 + y_r)$
$$(3.93) \quad (0.05) \qquad\qquad (0.56)$$
$$r^2 = 0.98.$$

The results definitely confirm the quantity theory—in both regressions the constant term is not significantly different from 0, and the value of the coefficient for the term in m is about 1 (marginally greater than 1 using the deflator). It is interesting to note that the fit for the deflator regression is slightly better than for the CPI regression, since in principle the deflator is a better overall measure of inflation; at the very least its coverage is defined over a broader class of goods and services. In both cases the coefficient for the term in y_r is negative, although not significant in the CPI regression. However, dropping the nonsignificant constant and reestimating through the origin yields significant estimates for all remaining coefficients:

Deflator: $\ln(1 + p) = 1.055 \ln(1 + m) -1.14 \ln(1 + y_r)$
$$(0.02) \qquad\qquad (0.139)$$
$$r^2 = 0.992$$

CPI: $\ln(1 + p) = 1.023 \ln(1 + m) -1.049 \ln(1 + y_r)$
$$(0.031) \qquad\qquad (0.217)$$
$$r^2 = 0.98.$$

The regressions for the deflator and the CPI show small differences, but the results are basically the same. Also, the explanatory power of the equations seems remarkably high—about as high as one can reasonably expect given

Table 1.2
Inflation, Monetary Growth, and Real Growth in Latin America, 1950–69
(average annual rates of change)

	Inflation	Monetary Growth	Real Growth
Uruguay	43.0	40.1	0.7
Bolivia	41.3	41.6	3.0
Brazil	35.1	38.2	3.9
Chile	28.2	35.2	4.6
Argentina	26.4	24.6	2.4
Paraguay	12.5	15.4	5.5
Colombia	9.2	16.5	5.4
Peru	8.5	13.4	5.7
Mexico	5.3	11.3	6.9
Nicaragua	3.4	8.6	3.7
Ecuador	3.0	8.8	4.7
Honduras	2.1	8.0	4.0
Costa Rica	1.9	9.0	5.7
Guatemala	1.1	5.9	3.9
Venezuela	1.1	7.9	6.8
El Salvador	0.3	3.5	4.6

Source: Vogel (1974), p. 103

the magnitude of the sampling errors inherent in measurements of inflation rates. (Note the sometimes quite large differences between inflation rates according to the two alternative indexes reported in Table 1.1.)

It is interesting to compare these results with the data presented by Vogel (1974), who computed the annual rates of inflation, monetary growth, and real growth for 16 Latin American countries in the period 1950–69. Vogel's data are summarized in Table 1.2 (inflation is measured by the CPI). Again, a clear relationship between price inflation and monetary growth is perceived. Estimating our regression equation with these data yields:

$$\ln(1 + p) = 0.061 + 1.075 \ln(1 + m) - 1.15 \ln(1 + y_r)$$
$$(2.04) \quad (0.047) \qquad\qquad (0.34)$$
$$r^2 = 0.983.$$

Dropping the nonsignificant constant and reestimating, we have

$$\ln(1 + p) = 1.075 \ln(1 + m) - 1.141 \ln(1 + y_r)$$
$$(0.028) \qquad\qquad (0.119)$$
$$r^2 = 0.984.$$

The results are basically the same, although some differences between the data in Table 1.1 and those in Table 1.2 should be pointed out.

1. The most obvious difference is that Vogel's sample includes Nicaragua but excludes the Dominican Republic, whereas Table 1.1 includes the Dominican Republic but excludes Nicaragua. The reason is that estimates of the CPI in Nicaragua for the period prior to 1975 are not available.
2. Vogel defines real output as Gross National Product deflated by the CPI. Table 1.1 shows statistics of real growth as reported by the World Bank in their *World Development Report 1982*, and which presumably have been computed by means of a more general deflator.
3. Whereas the data in Table 1.1 are average annual rates of change (the rate which when compounded annually is equivalent to total change over the period), the data in Table 1.2 are arithmetic averages of the annual rates of inflation, monetary growth, and real growth. That is, Table 1.1 reports "average annual rates," whereas Table 1.2 shows "averages of annual rates." These two measures are rarely equal, although differences are generally not too great.

It could be argued that the method of aggregating all Latin American countries "into a single equation" assumes away the existence of diverse "structural" factors peculiar to each country. However, the results seem to indicate that the structural factors are not very important—variations in the rate of monetary growth, and in the rate of real growth, explain practically all of the variation in the rate of inflation. (The structuralist theory of inflation is discussed in much greater detail in the following chapter.)

In both cases the estimated values of a_2 are less than -1 (although not significantly). In this regard the results are consistent with a large number of empirical studies that suggest that money is a luxury good in the sense that the income-elasticity of demand for money is greater than unity.[4] If this is the case in Latin America, then a_2 in our equation *should* be less than -1 (under the assumption adopted in the previous section of this chapter, $-a_2$ is in fact an estimator of the income-elasticity of demand for money). Relevant in this context is the well-known fact that statistics of national income are subject to large errors, especially in developing regions such as Latin America. Indeed, from recent research it is suggested that real income is seriously underestimated in these countries,[5] a factor that may imply that *rates* of real growth through time are somewhat overstated. If this is the case, then a regression using reported rates of real growth will tend to be biased toward lower (absolute) estimates of a_2.

The available data for the period since 1980 show essentially the same pattern summarized in Tables 1.1 and 1.2 and in the estimated regressions. To be sure, inflation accelerated in all but a few countries, in some cases reaching unheard of levels, but the difference is merely one of degree for accelerating inflation has been due to accelerating monetary growth. The relevant figures are shown in Table 1.3. Apart from the generally higher rates of monetary growth, recent experience differs from the previous decade in that rates of real growth have generally lowered (average real growth rates since 1980 have actually been *negative* in eight countries), but this has not altered the basic relationship between p, m, and y_r. Figure 1.1 compares the observed rates of (log-transformed) inflation during 1980–84 with the inflation rates predicted from the regression equation estimated for the 1970–80 data, given the observed rates of monetary and real growth during 1980–84 ("predicted" inflation is from the CPI regression). The observed inflation rates are denoted by the symbol +, while the predicted rates lie along the 45-degree straight line. In the case of high inflation countries, there is a visible tendency for inflation to exceed its predicted value. Actually, this is not surprising, since it is due to the effect of rising inflationary expectations. It is well known that in high inflation contexts the high real cost of holding money induces a "flight from currency" that aggravates the inflationary impact of additional monetary growth, and effectively reduces real money balances. Thus, prices rise at a faster rate than the money supply, resulting in a lower real money supply. What seems surprising, therefore, is not that observed inflation should exceed the rates warranted by observed monetary growth under the simple quantity theory model we have adopted so far, but rather the high rates of inflation at which this effect begins to have a detectable impact.

THE MONEY SUPPLY PROCESS IN LATIN AMERICA

It is frequently argued that the clear correlation between money and inflation does not imply anything about the direction of causality. Some authors feel that the money supply is the passive element in the relation, that it is not an independent variable. If the money supply increases, then this would be a simple "response" to inflation, not its cause. It is held, for instance, that in modern economies bank money—demand deposits, savings deposits—plays an important role, and that the volume of bank money is in some sense independent of the decisions of the monetary authorities, since it depends to a great extent upon the demand for bank loans, which could be affected by inflation. However, the available evidence indicates that, in practice, the greater share of monetary growth is due to factors that are, or can be, controllable by the monetary authorities, which implies that the greater share of monetary growth is due to factors that are, or can be, independent of the rate of inflation.

Table 1.3
Inflation, Monetary Growth, and Real Growth in Latin America, 1980-84
(average annual rates of change)

	Inflation	Monetary Growth	Real Growth
Argentina	316.6	259.5	- 1.6
Bolivia	369.1	287.1	- 4.6
Brazil	142.7	105.8	0.1
Chile	19.0	10.2	- 1.1
Colombia	21.2	23.4	2.0
Costa Rica	40.5	42.7	0.0
Dominican Republic	14.4	18.9	2.5
Ecuador	28.1	24.6	1.5
El Salvador	12.3	8.2	- 3.0
Guatemala	2.0	3.7	- 1.4
Honduras	8.1	8.5	0.4
Mexico	64.7	48.9	1.3
Paraguay	16.4	11.6	1.9
Peru	94.2	70.1	- 1.1
Uruguay	40.7	25.0	- 4.0
Venezuela	10.7	14.6	- 1.7

Sources: *Inflation*. Annualized change in the CPI from Dec 1980 to Dec 1984, computed from data reported in *International Financial Statistics*, Oct 1985, and "Supplement on Price Statistics," Supplement Series No. 2, 1981.

Monetary Growth. Annualized change in M_1 from Dec 1980 to Dec 1984, computed from data reported in *International Financial Statistics*, June 1986.

Real Growth. Annualized change in real GDP from 1980 to 1984, computed from data reported in *International Financial Statistics*, June 1986.

Conceptual Framework: Determinants of Monetary Growth

In the regression analyses of the previous section the money supply has been defined as the sum of currency outside banks (*C*) plus demand deposits in banks (D_d). With this definition it is commonly known as M_1. To identify the determinants of M_1 it is convenient to define an aggregate, known as the "monetary base" (*B*), which is the sum of currency outside banks plus the reserves of the banking system (*R*). Bank reserves consist of vault cash plus the deposits that banks hold in the central bank. Formally, the monetary base (sometimes also called "high-powered money") can be defined as

Figure 1.1
Latin American Inflation, 1980–84

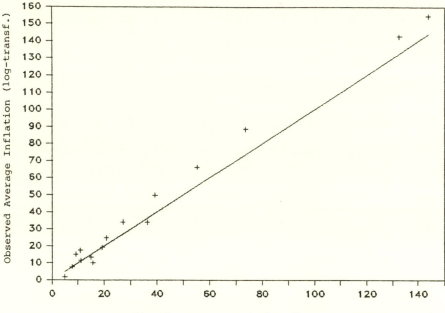

Predicted Average Inflation (log-transformed)

Source: Computed from data in Table 1.3.

"the kind of money which can be used as bank reserves." The concept is important because the central bank has direct control over the monetary base.[6] M_1 can be expressed as the product of the monetary base and a "multiplier" which depends upon, among other factors, the required reserve ratios that banks must hold against deposits, both demand and savings. From the definitions of M_1 and B we have

$$M_1 = C + D_d \tag{1.5}$$

$$B = C + R = C + RR + RE \tag{1.6}$$

where RR are the "required reserves" that banks must hold against deposits, and RE are the "excess reserves" that banks hold, where $RE = R - RR$. Define also the following ratios:

currency ratio $\qquad c = \dfrac{C}{D_d}$

savings ratio $\qquad s = \dfrac{D_s}{D_d}$

excess reserves ratio $\qquad e = \dfrac{RE}{D_d}$

where D_s are savings deposits in banks, and let r_d and r_s be the required reserve ratios on demand deposits and on savings deposits, respectively. Equations (1.5) and (1.6) can then be rewritten as

$$M_1 = cD_d + D_d = (1 + c)D_d \tag{1.5a}$$

$$B = cD_d + r_dD_d + r_sD_s + eD_d = (c + r_d + r_ss + e)D_d. \tag{1.6a}$$

Some algebra yields

$$M_1 = \left[\frac{1 + c}{c + r_d + r_s\,s + e} \right] B,$$

which establishes a direct relationship between M_1 and B. The expression in brackets is known as the "base-money multiplier," since it is the increase in M_1 which results from a unit increase in B. The stability of the relationship between M_1 and B depends upon the stability of the elements that determine the multiplier, which can be denoted as m_1. Clearly, a reduction in the required reserve ratios, r_d and r_s, will have a positive impact upon m_1, and therefore upon M_1, as will a reduction in s or in e. To evaluate the effect of a change in c, note that

$$\frac{\partial M_1}{\partial c} = \left[\frac{(c + r_d + r_s\,s + e) - (1 + c)}{(c + r_d + r_s\,s + e)^2} \right] B = \left[\frac{1 - m_1}{c + r_d + r_s\,s + e} \right] B < 0,$$

since, generally, $m_1 > 1$. Therefore, in general, M_1 will increase if the currency ratio, c, decreases.

Sources of Monetary Growth in Latin America, 1970–80

Following is an analysis of the determinants of monetary growth in Latin America in the period 1970–80. The basic data on M_1, the monetary base (B), bank reserves (R), demand deposits (D_d), and savings deposits (D_s) were obtained from *International Financial Statistics* (the well-known monthly statistical journal published by the International Monetary Fund). M_1 requires no further comments. The monetary base is in principle equal to the sum of currency outside banks plus the reserves of the banking system. (Alternatively, the base is the sum of total currency plus the deposits of the banking system in the central bank.) As a crude check of the consistency of each set of monetary aggregates, the reported data on B for each country were compared with implicit estimates of the monetary base using the relation:

$$B = M_1 - D_d + R.$$

In principle, both sets of figures should coincide exactly, although in practice discrepancies can arise owing to conceptual differences in the measurement of the aggregates, or there may be institutional differences between countries. In most cases the differences do not exceed $\pm 5\%$, and the only substantial difference arose in the data for Mexico, which would merit a more detailed analysis.

"Reserves" are the reserves of deposit banks (commercial banks and others with large demand deposits). Essentially, reserves are the sum of vault cash and deposits with the central bank. D_d are demand deposits and D_s are savings and term deposits in deposit banks.

Table 1.4 shows implicit estimates of m_1, the M_1 multiplier, computed as the ratio of M_1 to B. There is a high intercountry variation in m_1, doubtless owing to marked institutional differences. On the other hand, in most countries m_1 tends to be quite stable through time. Over the decade 1970–80, and with the single exception of Mexico, the average annual rate of change in the money multiplier did not exceed $\pm 4\%$ in any given country. These rates of change are very small, considering all the economic changes that took place during that decade, and especially when compared with the average annual rates of change in M_1 and B (see Table 1.5). The changes in B are always of the same order of magnitude as the changes in M_1, and at least one order of magnitude greater than the changes in m_1. In seven countries the changes in m_1 were negative, partly compensating the increases in B. In nine cases there was an increase in m_1, contributing to monetary growth, but invariably at least 90% of the increase in M_1 was due to the increase in B. Taking as significant a change greater than 1% per annum in absolute magnitude, we have six countries, over a third of the sample, that show no significant change in m_1 over the decade 1970–80. Of the nine countries that show an increase in m_1, only four show a significant increase.

Clearly, the greater share of monetary growth in Latin America was caused by changes in the monetary base. In the absence of changes in reserve requirements, the changes in m_1 could be interpreted as resulting from autonomous factors, beyond the control of the monetary authorities. However, there is reason to believe that not all of the variation in m_1 was due to autonomous factors, since changes in required reserve ratios have also contributed to the variation in m_1. To support this statement, without explicit documentation on changes in banking regulations, we can resort to indirect evidence.

Table 1.4
Monetary Multipliers in Latin America, 1970–80

	1970	1975	1980
Argentina	1.78	0.62	1.53
Bolivia	1.08	1.09	1.07
Brazil	1.90	2.34	1.95
Chile	1.30	0.83	0.87
Colombia	1.63	1.56	1.10
Costa Rica	1.69	1.68	1.23
Dominican Republic	0.95	0.98	1.02
Ecuador	1.33	1.43	1.59
El Salvador	0.98	1.02	1.15
Guatemala	1.09	1.03	1.11
Honduras	1.42	1.59	1.58
Mexico	1.84	0.87	0.66
Paraguay	0.85	0.82	0.87
Peru	1.17	1.17	0.84
Uruguay	1.11	0.97	1.22
Venezuela	1.70	1.73	1.92

Source: Computed from data reported in *International Financial Statistics*, Dec 1977, Dec 1982, and Yearbook 1984. (M_1—line 34; Monetary Base—line 14.)

Consider the "reserve ratio," r, given by

$$r = \frac{R}{D_d + D_s}.$$

In our simplied framework we have

$$r = \frac{r_d D_d + r_s D_s + RE}{D_d + D_s} = \frac{r_d + r_s s + e}{1 + s}$$

where the notation has been defined above. The reserves ratio depends essentially upon the required reserve ratios and upon s, the savings ratio, since e is generally a small number. In practice the situation could be somewhat more complicated, since in many countries there are different required reserve ratios for different kinds of banks. For instance, both r_d and r_s could be different for private banks and for public sector banks, or for

Table 1.5
Determinants of Monetary Growth in Latin America
(average annual rates of change, 1970–80)

	M_1	B	m_1
Argentina	114.2	117.4	− 1.5
Bolivia	25.4	25.5	− 0.1
Brazil	44.2	43.8	0.2
Chile	145.3	155.3	− 3.9
Colombia	25.2	30.2	− 3.8
Costa Rica	21.9	25.8	− 3.1
Dominican Republic	12.9	12.1	0.7
Ecuador	24.5	22.3	1.8
El Salvador	17.1	15.2	1.6
Guatemala	15.8	15.7	0.2
Honduras	14.4	13.1	1.1
Mexico	24.4	37.8	− 9.7
Paraguay	23.9	23.6	0.2
Peru	33.1	37.6	− 3.2
Uruguay	60.0	57.5	0.9
Venezuela	22.2	20.8	1.2

Source: Computed from data reported in *International Financial Statistics*, Dec 1977, Dec
1982, and Yearbook 1984. (M_1—line 34; Monetary Base—line 14.)

domestic banks and foreign banks. Therefore, even with constant required
reserve and savings ratios, r could change as a result of a change in the
distribution of deposits among different kinds of banks. Also, there are
other types of deposits that are sometimes subject to reserve requirements,
such as term deposits. On the other hand, the differences between required
reserve ratios for different kinds of banks are much smaller than the differences between required reserve ratios for different types of deposits, and
the greater share of bank deposits are demand and savings deposits. Consequently, the expression or r as a function of r_d, r_s, and s will be a good approximation in most cases. A substantial change in r implies a change in the
required reserve ratios, in the savings ratio, or in all three.

Table 1.6 shows the percentage changes in r and s over the period 1970–80
for the ten countries which show significant changes in m_1 over the same
period. Note that

Table 1.6
Percentage Change in Reserves and Savings Ratios, 1970–80

	Reserves Ratio	Savings Ratio	Implicit Change in Reserve Requirements	Observed Change in m_1
Argentina	-29.1	353.7	+ (?)	-
Chile	-19.9	352.0	+ (?)	-
Colombia	53.7	304.7	+	-
Costa Rica	7.6	283.7	+	-
Ecuador	-7.5	-53.4	-	+
El Salvador	-22.1	-14.1	-	+
Honduras	-23.4	1.3	-	+
Mexico	92.7	453.6	+	-
Peru	35.8	180.5	+	-
Venezuela	-24.9	2.8	-	+

Source: Computed from data reported in *International Financial Statistics*, Dec 1977, Dec 1982, and Yearbook 1984. (Bank Reserves—line 20; Demand Deposits—line 24; Savings and Term Deposits—line 25.)

$$\frac{\partial r}{\partial s} = \frac{r_s - r}{1 + s} < 0,$$

since r_s is always less than r_d and is therefore less than r, which amounts to a weighted average of r_d and r_s. That is, an increase in s causes a decrease in r, and a decrease in s causes an increase in r, if required reserve ratios do not change. Therefore, an increase in s that is not followed by a decrease in r implies an increase in required reserve ratios—this is the case for Colombia, Costa Rica, Mexico, and Peru. Similarly, a decrease in s not followed by an increase in r implies a decrease in required reserve ratios—the case for Ecuador and El Salvador. (Perhaps it should be pointed out that these predictions are strictly valid only for substantial changes in s, since changes in e might act as a slack variable in the case of relatively small changes. The observed changes in s, however, seem prima facie sufficiently "substantial" to warrant the conclusions.) Finally, note that the elasticity of r with respect to s is

$$e(r, s) = \frac{\partial r}{\partial s} \cdot \frac{s}{r} = \frac{s}{1 + s} \left(\frac{r_s}{r} - 1 \right).$$

Clearly, $-1 < e(r, s) < 0$, that is, a 1% change in s will cause a less than 1% change in r, with opposite sign, if required reserve ratios are constant. Therefore, if the changes in r and in s are of opposite sign, and the percentage change in r is greater than the percentage change in s, then this implies that a change in required reserve ratios has occurred in the same direction as the change in r. This is the case of Honduras and Venezuela, which show implicit decreases in required reserve ratios. The cases of Argentina and Chile are somewhat less clear than the others, but to judge from the magnitude of the changes in s, and the relatively small decline in r, it seems apparent that required reserve ratios have been increased in those countries.

The indirect evidence of Table 1.6 suggests that all countries that show significant changes in m_1 also show changes in required reserve ratios. (The exact magnitude of these changes can be determined only by an historical study of the evolution of banking regulations in each country. However, the information contained in the reserves and savings ratios is sufficient to determine the existence and direction of a change.) Also, in all cases the changes in required reserve ratios and those in m_1 are of opposite signs, that is, the changes have not been compensating but rather have *reinforced* the trends in m_1 caused by autonomous factors. Therefore, at least part of the variation in m_1 was due to changes in required reserve ratios, which are controlled by the monetary authorities. The variations in m_1 would have been smaller had these controllable factors been held constant.

Though the preceding analysis seems quite conclusive, it is possibly superfluous in light of certain results reported by Fama (1982), who suggests that the relevant aggregate for the control of inflation is not M_1 but the monetary base itself. If the quantity theory is correct, and if M_1 is the relevant monetary aggregate, then the two components of the rate of change in M_1 should be symmetrical in their separate effects upon the rate of inflation. That is, in the regression

$$\ln(1 + p) = b_1 \ln(1 + b) + b_2 \ln(1 + m_1) + b_3 \ln(1 + y_r)$$

where b and m_1 represent the average annual rates of change in the monetary base and in the M_1 multiplier, respectively, the coefficients for the terms in b and m_1 should be equal and about 1. Estimating this regression with the data in Tables 1.1 and 1.5 yields the following results:

Deflator: $\ln(1 + p) = 1.058 (1 + b) + 1.087 \ln(1 + m_1) - 1.146 \ln(1 + y_r)$
$\qquad\qquad\quad (0.023) \qquad\quad (0.214) \qquad\qquad (0.148)$
$$r^2 = 0.992$$

$$CPI: \ln(1 + p) = 1.028 \ln(1 + b) + 1.133 \ln(1 + m_1) - 1.054 \ln(1 + y_r)$$
$$(0.035)(0.332)(0.23)$$
$$r^2 = 0.979$$

Although the coefficients for the terms in b and m_1 are roughly equal in both regressions, the estimates for the m_1 coefficients, although significant, are much less significant than those for the b and y_r coefficients. This would tend to confirm Fama's contention, although it could also be a purely statistical result due to the small in-sample variation in m_1 rates of change, and a definite conclusion is not warranted at this stage.

NOTES

1. See, for example, Martino (1981). Prof. Martino argues convincingly that the rapid rise in recent years in the ratio of money supply to official GNP in Italy is a reflection of the growth in the unofficial—or "underground"—economy, which of course fails to show up in the official national income statistics. Martino concluded that the official data tend to seriously underestimate real national income. It is interesting to note that the Italian statistical authority, though it at first denied the possibility of an underestimation, later confirmed this interpretation by revising upwards its previous official GNP estimates by 10 percent!

Since real income generally varies within relatively narrow ranges, a substantial and rapid rise in the money/income ratio implies a substantial and rapid rise in the real money supply, that is, rates of growth in the (nominal) money supply substantially in excess of rates of price inflation. This is a rare phenomenon. In fact, a reasonably exhaustive survey of the published record affords only two well-documented cases, namely, the German experience during World War II (Klein, 1956), and the trends in certain Middle Eastern countries studied by Penrose (1962). Even these cases are less than conclusive, however, since the German experience is to some extent a reflection of pervasive price controls, while Penrose's data suffer from severe measurement problems in the price indexes.

2. In general, the elasticity of x with respect to y, which we can denote by the expression $e(x, y)$, is defined as the proportional change in x caused by a 1% change in y. Mathematically, $e(x, y)$ is defined as

$$e(x, y) = \frac{\partial x}{\partial y} \cdot \frac{y}{x} = \frac{\partial \ln x}{\partial \ln y} \ .$$

Denote nominal money supply and income by M and Y, respectively, and real money supply and income by M_r and Y_r, respectively ($M_r = M/P$ and $Y_r = Y/P$, where P is the relevant price deflator). Finally, denote the ratio of money to income by $k = M/Y = M_r/Y_r$. Based on empirical evidence, it is quite clear that a change in real income will induce an increase in real money balances, though the change in the *ratio* of money to income will depend upon the magnitude of the income elasticity. It is easily shown that

$$\frac{\partial \ln k}{\partial \ln Y_r} = \frac{\partial \ln M_r}{\partial \ln Y_r} - 1 = e(M_r, Y_r) - 1.$$

If $e(M_r, Y_r) > 1$, then k will increase with real income. In this case money could be described as a "luxury" good as the public will hold a larger fraction of increasing income in the form of money. If $0 < e(M_r, Y_r) < 1$, then the demand for money will rise with real income, but less than proportionally, so k will decrease. This would be described as a case of "economies of scale" in the use of money balances, as the public would hold a smaller fraction of their (increasing) incomes in the form of money. The possibility that $e(M_r, Y_r) < 0$ is of course ruled out on empirical grounds.

3. In this context it is well to note that the heavy emphasis on interest rates in the U.S. studies is possibly misplaced. In any case, if following the well-known Fisher equation the nominal interest rate is viewed as the sum of a real interest rate and expected inflation, then the use of interest rates will in fact measure the effect of changes in inflationary expectations insofar as variations in the real rate of interest can be expected to be relatively minor.

4. For instance, Friedman (1959), who uses U.S. data and obtains an elasticity of 1.8. The income-elasticity of money demand in developing countries has been the focus of several recent studies (see Crockett and Evans, 1980, and literature cited therein). Given the obvious data limitations, the results naturally vary across countries, but a more or less consistent finding is that the estimated elasticities are generally between 1 and 1.5.

5. For example, see Kravis (1984). The classic analysis of the limitations of economic statistics is that by Morgenstern (1963)—see especially his chapters 14 and 15.

6. See Balbach (1981). This statement is necessarily true in an accounting sense, although the extent to which the authorities can actually control the base may depend upon legal-institutional factors. For instance, if the central bank has a rediscount policy, then the base will depend upon the demand for rediscounts by the commercial banks, which cannot be directly controlled by the monetary authorities. Similarly, under a system of fixed exchange rates the monetary base is affected by fluctuations in international trade and capital flows, since the central bank is committed to sell and purchase a certain foreign currency at a certain rate of exchange. If the country has a surplus balance of payments, then the difference between the supply and demand of foreign currency must be absorbed by the central bank through purchases financed by increases in the monetary base. In this situation, the authorities cannot have strict control over the monetary base (in fact, this was the situation of countries such as Japan and West Germany in the late 1960s, which eventually forced them to abandon the system of fixed exchange rates in 1973). In the case of Latin America, the base-money effects of the huge growth in the external debt of that region over the decade under consideration were not negligible. The limitations to base-money control in small very open economies under fixed exchange rates are well known, and flexible exchange rates have long been proposed as a means of enhancing the degree of domestic monetary control.

CHAPTER 2

AN ALTERNATIVE VIEW: THE STRUCTURALIST ARGUMENT REVISITED

Rapid inflation has been conspicuous in several Latin American countries for the past few decades. Efforts to explain this persistent phenomenon in terms of features common to most Latin American economies led to an interpretation that departed from what was described as the "orthodox," or monetary, approach. The new view, perhaps for lack of a better term, was labeled "structuralism," and much of its literature shared a controversial tone, developed as it was in the heat of criticism of perceived orthodoxy, though to speak of a structuralist-monetarist debate is something of a misnomer, since there was actually very little detailed criticism of the structuralist theses from the monetarist perspective. (For a notable exception see Campos, 1961; see also the papers collected in the volume edited by Baer and Kerstenetzky, 1964).

Whatever debate there was may be said to have concluded, more or less inconclusively, by the mid-1960s. By that time all of the classic structuralist papers had been published, and since then there have been few analytical contributions to the literature.[1] On the other hand, there has been a steady flow of criticism of the monetarist view at the policy level, particularly over the last decade and motivated especially by the ostensibly monetarist-inspired policy experiments in the Southern Cone.[2]

The failure of these policies does not, of course, necessarily invalidate the monetarist *analysis*, nor does it in itself vindicate the structuralist argument, though in many circles the situation is in fact thusly interpreted. The purpose of this chapter is therefore to "revisit" the controversy so as to clearly delineate the analytical differences between the opposing views, and to review the evidence pertaining to them.

AN OVERVIEW

Osvaldo Sunkel's analysis of the Chilean inflation was probably the first presentation of the structuralist theory as a unified whole, an interpretation that he explicitly contrasted with the "orthodox" approach. As he phrases it, the Chilean inflation—as that of other countries with similar degree of development, similar economic structure, and comparable historical evolution—must be analyzed in the light of an *own* interpretation, conditioned by the reality to which it purports to apply.

According to this new interpretation,

the underlying sources of inflation in underdeveloped countries are to be found in the basic problems of economic development, in the structural characteristics which the productive system of these countries exhibits (Sunkel, 1958, p. 571, emphasis added).

The new approach must go beyond the traditional analysis, which does no more than "display accusingly the now classic monetary statistics," and in the best of cases only allows to trace the course of inflation in the financial sphere, without managing however to "explain its causes, its persistence, nor its local characteristics." The objective, therefore, is to explain inflation by reference to its "ultimate causes." Since these are admittedly manifold, what is needed is an analytical framework which will allow to "disentangle from among all the causal elements those which are primary and those which play a secondary role" (Sunkel, 1958, p. 572).

From the outset Sunkel distinguishes the diverse inflationary pressures from what he calls the propagation mechanism. He is at pains to stress this distinction, which the monetary view apparently overlooks, as they constitute "different logical categories." The latter cannot cause inflation, though it may maintain it, or even aggravate it. Moreover, it is "the most visible aspect of the inflationary mechanism," which commonly leads it to be confused with the "true causes of inflation."

These in turn are classified in three broad categories: (a) basic, or "structural" pressures, (b) "circumstantial" pressures, and (c) "cumulative" pressures induced by the inflationary process itself. The second category of circumstantial factors consists of what might be called "random shocks" (for example, exogenous increases in import prices, natural disasters, etc.), and although it is part and parcel of the overall structuralist view, it is not easily amenable to theoretical analysis, and does not play an important role in the theory.[3]

The leading role is that of the first category, the basic factors, which according to Sunkel are due to

limitations, rigidities, or inflexibilities of the economic system. In effect, the inability of certain productive sectors to adapt to changes in demand . . . the low mobility of productive resources and a deficient price system, are the main generator(s) of structural inflationary disequilibria (1958, pp. 573-74).

He refers specifically to (1) the slow response of agricultural output in the face of increasing demand, (2) the uneven growth of export revenues (capacity to import) in the face of increasing demand for imports, (3) insufficient capital formation, and, interestingly enough, (4) structural deficiencies in the tax system.

Sunkel deals with each of these factors in the Chilean context, but he seems to stress especially the first two, and in this he has been followed by most other writers in the structuralist tradition. Indeed, the twin problems of the low supply-elasticity of farm output and the "import bottleneck" may be said to form the core of the structuralist analysis. (Other factors, such as inadequate infrastructure facilities, are sometimes added to the list of basic factors, though they generally play a subordinate role in the analysis; see, however, Guzmán, 1974).

Though Sunkel's taxonomy seems logically complete, it is not as airtight as may seem at first glance. For instance, in practice it is hard to distinguish the propagation mechanism, which consists essentially of the public sector deficit, from Sunkel's fourth structural factor (rigid tax system), or from one of the several "cumulative" pressures.[4]

It is significant, in passing, that the analysis at this stage bears a striking resemblance to the much criticized orthodox approach. Thus, "one of the principal agents in the propagation of inflationary pressures of all types lies in the method of financing the public sector, which leads inevitably to currency issues."[5] In fact, the discussion of propagating factors by structuralist authors is generally consistent with the traditional monetary analysis, but the issue in their view is why the need for monetary expansion arises in the first place. To delve deeper into the differences in the opposing views we therefore return to the basic factors for further scrutiny.

Low Price-responsiveness in Key Sectors

This factor has been stressed in every major statement of the structuralist viewpoint, and recent formulations (for example, Canavese, 1982) have added very little to the general argument. Emphasis has been placed on the agricultural sector, though the argument can be generalized to encompass any sector in which rigidities lead to a buildup of pressures from the real side during the process of economic growth. Basically, because of alleged supply inelasticities in agriculture (which are held to be closely related to systems of land tenure), the increase in demand for food products resulting from rising incomes in other sectors, as well as from population growth and the increasing urbanization that accompanies economic development, will tend to push up the relative price of food. Since absolute prices are postulated to be inflexible downwards, relative price increases in some sectors will tend to translate into increases in the general price level. This "ratchet effect" of relative price changes was formalized by Olivera (1960), in what he called a "non-monetary theory of inflation." (Olivera's analysis is similar to the theory formulated by Schultze (1959), though his formal argument is somewhat more rigorous than Schultze's). Given the assumptions of the theory, a positive and persistent rate of inflation is therefore theoretically possible even in the absence of changes in the money supply.[6] One may question, however, the need for a strictly nonmonetary theory given the well-known fact that high inflation countries *always* exhibit high rates of monetary growth (which are moreover highly correlated with rates of price inflation). On the other hand, the underlying "ratchet" inflation may explain the pressure placed upon the monetary authorities to expand the money supply in the context of a completely passive monetary policy (see Olivera, 1971).

The Import Bottleneck

This factor also plays an essential role in structuralist theory. According to this argument, the demand for imports, which is highly income-elastic in Latin American countries, will tend to rise in the course of economic growth, outstripping the capacity to import from export revenues, which need not rise pari passu with import demand, and generally will not do so. Indeed, the supply of exports is viewed as inelastic, at least in the short run, and the resulting "import bottleneck" places a binding constraint upon the possibilities for economic growth, which depends more upon the ability to finance needed imports than upon the rate of domestic savings. Furthermore, the excess demand for imports will place pressure upon the exchange rate, and the resulting devaluations will in turn tend to increase the internal price level.

This situation is in itself sufficient to guarantee chronic import inflation. It can be aggravated by some complementary scenarios that are often postulated in this context (but that are not essential to the argument). For instance, the situation will be still worse if, in addition, exports are subject to declining terms of trade. The import bottleneck is also often combined with "elasticity pessimism" (in the sense of the Marshall-Lerner stability conditions), whereby the resulting devaluations are viewed as having virtually no effect in reducing the excess demand for imports—inelastic exports and relatively price-inelastic demand for imports—so the net effect is simply an increase in the cost of imports.

EMPIRICAL EVIDENCE

Whatever one may think of the foregoing arguments, it is clear that the "basic" factors become operative only in the presence of real economic growth, which in this context is taken as given—the deus ex machina that more or less moves the process. As stated, therefore, the structuralist theories would imply that inflationary pressures should be absent in a low growth environment. In fact, the analysis would preclude the existence of inflation in such situations. Likewise, if the analysis is interpreted strictu sensu, inflation should inevitably accompany high rates of economic growth given the structural rigidities that are allegedly a characteristic of Latin American economies generally. The structuralist theory therefore implies, at least "on average" or in some long-run sense, a positive relationship between inflation and rates of real economic growth. Even the most cursory examination of the empirical data, however, reveals that the Latin American economies exhibit the full range of possible combinations of inflation and growth (see Figure 2.1). It anything, the long-run data would point toward a negative, albeit rather loose, relation.

Though such casual empiricism is usually rejected, even derided, in the structuralist literature, the hard fact remains, however, that the cases of low inflation countries with persistently high growth rates is a basic anomaly in terms of structuralist theory. (On the other hand, they are perfectly consistent with the monetarist view, which postulates no relation whatsoever between inflation and economic growth in the long run.) These cases thus constitute prima facie evidence that the structuralist theory is at the very least somewhat lacking in generality.

Before going on to detailed empirical analysis of the evidence regarding specific elements of the structuralist theory (such as the role of food prices and the import bottleneck), it is well to clarify an issue that has been a source of misunderstanding. Though structuralists hold that inflation is an inevitable by-product of economic growth in Latin American-type economies, they do not generally argue that it is a necessary condition for growth, much less that it is conducive to growth, a view that is sometimes imputed to them. The question as to whether inflation may in fact stimulate economic growth is nonetheless an interesting one in its own right. As a result of Johnson's (1984) penetrating investigation of the matter, it turns out that this depends upon a highly restrictive set of conditions that need not necessarily hold. It is not surprising, therefore, that early studies—for example, Tun Wai (1959), Dorrance (1966)—failed to find any detectable relation between growth and inflation. More recently, Agarwala (1983) has found some evidence of a negative effect of inflation on real economic growth, but again the relationship is a rather weak one, and there are exceptions. In Latin America the most obvious exception is the case of Brazil during the 1970s, a high inflation country with a consistently strong growth record. Upon closer examination, however, the Brazilian case may be consistent with Agarwala's characterization of the process that underlies the observed

Figure 2.1
Growth and Inflation in Latin America

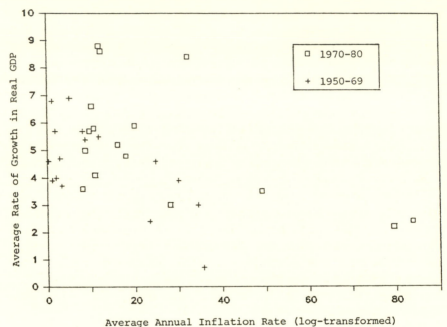

Source: Based on data in Tables 1.1 and 1.2.

negative relationship between inflation and growth. In effect, Agarwala
argues convincingly that distortions in relative prices have a growth-inhibiting
effect. Since inflation often results in seriously distorted relative prices in
labor markets, in the financial and credit system, and in the pricing of public
utilities and government services, it is likely that the negative effect of inflation on growth is not due to the inflation itself, but to inflation-induced price
distortions. The Brazilian experience, however, has not been typical in this
regard, since Brazil is the only country in Latin America with a fully
developed and consistently applied system of indexation for inflation. See,
for example, Kafka (1974), and Fishlow (1974). To evaluate the full impact of
indexation upon the economic performance of the Brazilian economy is of
course a well nigh impossible task, but it seems quite clear that the system has
at the very least allowed the economy to avoid the worst of the price distortions usually induced by inflation in developing economies.

Food Prices and Inflation

In examining the available evidence regarding the role of food prices in the generation of inflation, a useful starting point is Griffin's succinct summary statement of the structuralist view:

> [I]f food output does not increase at the same rate as additional demand, while population and industrial output grow, agricultural prices—in the absence of effective controls—will rise. The increase in urban incomes, resulting from increased industrial output, will soon lead to an increase in food prices. This will raise the cost of living, which will put pressure upon wages. This can easily result, at this point, in a spiral movement from the higher cost of living, to higher wages, and higher prices in general (1972, p. 204).

A clear empirical implication of this characterization of the inflation-generating process is that high inflation countries should exhibit a rising trend in the real price of food products. Surprisingly, given the important role of rising food prices in the structuralist explanation, most formulations have tended to neglect empirical analysis of the actual evolution of real food prices in Latin America. Sunkel's original analysis of the Chilean inflation is a notable exception, but since then most structuralist writers (when they appeal to empirical evidence at all) have rested their case on the analysis of indexes of agricultural production rather than looking at prices directly (for example, Griffin, 1972, p. 205).

Table 2.1 shows the evolution of relative food prices (measured by the food price component of the CPI, deflated by the total CPI) in 16 Latin American countries since 1960. Overall, the general trend in the real price of food products over the entire period 1960–84 has been upward in all but five countries. Interestingly enough, one of the exceptions, Uruguay, has traditionally been a high inflation country—persistent inflation in Uruguay can hardly have been generated by a wage-price spiral originating in rising real food prices.

The secular rise in the relative price of food products in much of Latin America is an interesting phenomenon in its own right, the explanation of which, for all we know, may very well lie in the factors stressed by structuralist theory. The relevant question, however, is whether or not the observed increase in real food prices is somehow related to inflation in general. In fact, these phenomena do not appear to be related at all.

To begin with, though the change in real food prices over the full period 1960–84 has generally been a net increase, in most countries the trend has not been an unbroken upward movement. In fact, only three countries—Costa Rica, Ecuador, and Venezuela—show a consistent upward trend in real food prices for the full period 1960–84 as well as for the three subperiods considered in Table 2.1. Needless to say, these are not high inflation countries. The case of Uruguay is of course the exact opposite. However, these are not

Table 2.1
Real Food Prices in Latin America, 1960-84

	Indices (1970 = 100)			Percentage Change			
	1960	1980	1984	1960-70	1970-80	1980-84	1960-84
Argentina	105.5	103.5	106.6	-5.2	3.5	3.0	1.0
Bolivia	105.6	108.7	122.7	-5.3	8.7	12.9	16.2
Brazil	115.4	117.9	134.1	-13.3	17.9	13.7	16.2
Chile	90.5	119.4	107.2	10.5	19.4	-10.2	18.4
Colombia	99.1	121.9	123.9	0.9	21.9	1.6	25.0
Costa Rica	94.9	108.8	118.1	5.4	8.8	8.5	24.4
Dominican Republic	102.2	102.8	93.9	-2.1	2.8	-8.6	-8.1
Ecuador	86.1	116.4	153.9	16.1	16.4	32.2	78.7
El Salvador	100.0	97.7	101.5	0.0	-2.3	3.9	1.5
Guatemala	99.1	93.9	90.4	0.9	-6.1	-3.7	-8.7
Honduras	101.8	108.3	95.9	-1.7	8.3	-11.4	-5.7
Mexico	103.2	101.7	96.4	-3.1	1.7	-5.2	-6.6
Paraguay	97.8	112.7	109.3(n)	2.2	12.7	-3.0(n)	11.7(n)
Peru	105.0	116.2	114.0	-4.8	16.2	-1.9	8.6
Uruguay	115.4	94.0	92.9	-13.3	-6.0	-1.2	-19.5
Venezuela	97.8	138.1	151.4	2.2	38.1	9.6	54.8

Note: The index corresponds to 1983, and the percentage change is for 1980-83, and for 1960-83.
Source: Computed from data reported in *Statistical Yearbook for Latin America and the Caribbean*, 1985 Edition (Santiago, Chile: United Nations, 1986). The index of real food prices is defined as the food component of the CPI deflated by the total CPI.

the only cases which, to say the least, do not admit a structuralist interpretation. The experience of the 1960s is particularly damaging for the structuralist viewpoint (which is all the more surprising, since much of the early structuralist literature dates from that period). In fact, of the five traditionally high inflation countries (Argentina, Brazil, Chile, Peru, and Uruguay) only Chile shows an increase in real food prices during that decade; food prices actually declined in real terms in the other high inflation countries.

The Impact of Import Inflation

The argument based on the import bottleneck implicitly assumes a direct and significant relationship between import costs and internal prices. Indeed, the validity of the whole argument depends on such a link, which is more or less taken for granted, and rarely if ever tested directly. Given the importance of such a postulate for the general structuralist argument, the relative lack of detailed statistical studies of the impact of import costs on domestic inflation is rather surprising. In fact, such studies are virtually unheard of in the Latin American context, with the notable exception of a recent study by Galbis (1982), who approached the problem within the framework of a linear decomposition of the sources of domestic inflation:

$$p = \beta(p_e + r) + (1 - \beta)p_i \qquad\qquad (2.1)$$

where, in keeping with our previous notation, p is the rate of inflation. The first term of this expression, the inflation due to external sources, depends in turn on two factors: p_e, the rate of increase in import prices (in U.S. dollar terms), and r, the percentage devaluation in the exchange rate (expressed in terms of domestic currency per U.S. dollar). The joint effect of these two factors determines the rate of increase in the cost of imports in terms of domestic currency, which is weighted by the ratio of total imports to Gross Domestic Product, β, since changes in the cost of imports will have a greater impact, ceteris paribus, the larger the share of imports in the total GDP. The second term of the expression represents the inflation due to internal sources.

Galbis presented estimates of the inflation imputable to external factors for eight Latin American countries over the period 1973–79, which are summarized in Table 2.2. The data clearly show that, particularly in high inflation countries, the external factors contribute only marginally toward the explanation of domestic inflation. The inflation originating in internal sources, estimated as a residual, in most cases represents by far the larger share. Data covering a longer time span and a larger group of countries are reported in Table 2.3, which shows essentially the same picture.

Table 2.2
External and Internal Factors in Domestic Inflation, 1973–79
(average annual rates of change)

	Consumer Price Index	External Factors	Internal Factors (Residual)
Argentina	168.1	28.5	139.6
Bolivia	17.6	5.2	12.4
Chile	161.2	32.7	128.5
Colombia	23.3	3.9	19.4
Costa Rica	11.5	7.8	3.7
Mexico	19.8	3.9	15.9
Peru	37.0	12.9	24.1
Venezuela	8.5	2.9	5.6

Source: Computed from data reported in Galbis (1982), Table 2, p. 25. (The original yearly data were averaged over the sample period.)

This statistical approach is perhaps overly rigid, as it assumes that import inflation affects internal prices only in proportion to the relative magnitude of imports in the GDP. It is possible, on the other hand, that external factors might transmit an inflationary impulse to the internal factors. In fact, Galbis points out that equation (2.1) yields "an estimate of the minimum effect of the increase in foreign prices upon internal prices" (1982, p. 23). Therefore, the impact of external factors should be estimated within the framework of a general explanatory model of inflation.

We have shown in Chapter 1 that a simple linear regression of the form

$$\ln(1 + p) = a_1\ln(1 + m) + a_2\ln(1 + y_r)$$

explains the larger share of the cross-country variation in average annual rates of inflation, where m and y_r represent the average annual rates of monetary growth and real GDP growth, respectively. If changes in import costs in fact contribute to domestic inflation, then the addition of an import cost variable to this regression equation should significantly increase its explanatory power. Therefore a direct test of the import-inflation hypothesis would be the estimation of

$$\ln(1 + p) = a_1\ln(1 + m) + a_2\ln(1 + y_r) + a_3\beta\ln(1 + p_m)$$

Table 2.3
External and Internal Factors in Domestic Inflation, 1970–80
(average annual rates of exchange)

	Consumer Price Index	External Factors		Internal Factors (Residual)
		Import Price Deflator	Imports/GDP (percent)	
Chile	131.2	157.1	22.9	95.2
Argentina	121.4	107.9	8.5	112.2
Uruguay	63.5	64.1	17.8	52.1
Brazil	38.1	45.4	9.6	33.7
Peru	32.5	36.3	18.6	25.7
Bolivia	19.7	24.4	23.3	14.0
Colombia	22.1	21.0	14.1	19.1
Mexico	17.5	17.0	10.4	15.7
Costa Rica	11.3	14.0	38.1	6.0
Ecuador	12.6	15.6	26.5	8.5
Paraguay	13.1	10.6	17.7	11.2
El Salvador	11.5	11.6	34.1	7.5
Guatemala	10.1	14.4	23.8	6.7
Dominican Republic	10.7	8.3	26.0	8.5
Honduras	8.4	9.3	37.7	4.9

Note: Column (4) = Column (1) minus Column (2) × Column (3).

Sources: *Inflation*. See Table 1.1.

 Import Prices. Computed from implicit deflators derived from data on total imports in current and constant prices, as reported in *Statistical Yearbook for Latin America and the Caribbean*, 1985 Edition (Santiago, Chile: United Nations, 1986). Venezuela not available.

 Import Shares (β). Average share of imports in GDP, 1971–80 (Chile, 1973–80), computed from data reported in *International Financial Statistics*, "Supplement on Output Statistics," Supplement Series No. 8, 1984.

where p_m represents the average annual rate of increase in import prices (in terms of domestic currency), which is weighted by β, the share of imports in the GDP. If the import-inflation hypothesis is valid, then $a_3 > 0$. On the other hand, if inflation essentially depends upon internal monetary and real factors, then p_m should not have a significant effect, that is, $a_3 = 0$, since changes in relative prices (for example, changes in import costs) will not affect general inflation.[7]

This regression equation was estimated with the data in Tables 1.1 and 2.3 (import inflation is measured by the import price deflator, which implicitly includes both increases in import unit values as well as exchange rate variations). Ordinary least squares yields:

Deflator: $\ln(1 + p) = 1.097 \ln(1 + m) - 1.11 \ln(1 + y_r) - 0.239 \ \beta\ln(1 + p_m)$
$(0.04) \qquad\qquad (0.13) \qquad\qquad (0.20)$

$$r^2 = 0.994$$

CPI: $\ln(1 + p) = \quad 1.13 \ln(1 + m) \ -1.02 \ln(1 + y_r) \ -0.646 \ \beta\ln(1 + p_m)$
$(0.051) \qquad\qquad (0.167) \qquad\qquad (0.258)$

$$r^2 = 0.99.$$

The estimated coefficients for the terms in m and y_r are significant and consistent with their theoretical values ($a_1 = 1$, $a_2 < 0$), whereas the coefficient for the term in p_m does not even have the expected sign.

To summarize, these results clearly indicate that, as far as the Latin American experience is concerned, there is no evidence whatsoever in favor of the proposition that import costs contribute to domestic inflation. Plausible as that intuition may seem, import prices have had no statistically detectable effect upon Latin American inflation, which has been due exclusively to internal factors.

NOTES

1. Any list of landmark papers must per force include those by Sunkel (1958), Seers (1962), Olivera (1964), Prebisch (1961), and Grunwald (1961). The first three papers were later reprinted as a single volume: Sunkel et al. (1967). A useful survey of the early structuralist literature is that by Baer (1967). The general survey articles by Bronfenbrenner and Holzman (1963), Bronfenbrenner (1968), and Frisch (1977) include brief discussions of the structuralist point of view, and the review article by Padvalskis-Simkus (1967) is also helpful. To a greater or lesser extent, more recent papers simply restate and refine the original formulations. Noteworthy, however, is a structuralist analysis of "stagflation" by Olivera (1980). The analysis is usually limited to developing economies, and is often presented within the framework of the general theory of underdevelopment associated with CEPAL (UN Economic Commission for Latin America)—for example, Rodriguez (1979)—though one leading exponent (Pinto, 1975) has felt confident enough in the structuralist analysis to apply it to inflation in the developed economies as well.

2. See, for instance, Ferrer (1981), Ffrench-Davis (1983), and Fortín (1984). The monetarist analysis is also often associated with the policies of the International Monetary Fund, which have been much criticized throughout the region. (There is an element of guilt by association of words here, "monetarismo" of course being associated with "fondomonetarismo," which in turn, to put it bluntly, has rightly or wrongly become something akin to a cussword in many circles.)

3. They are, however, usually taken into account in applied analyses of concrete

situations. The first OPEC oil shock, for instance, plays an important role in Latin American inflation in the period 1972-74 according to Assael and Núñez del Prado (1976).

4. Viz., in the section on cumulative pressures: "In the public sector, expectations of increasing wages and prices determines the corresponding increase in the budget, if only to attempt to maintain the public sector's real share in the national expenditure" (Sunkel, 1958, p. 585).

5. Sunkel, 1958, p. 587. Likewise, in the discussion of cumulative pressures Sunkel argues, in effect, that inflationary expectations will lead to an increase in the velocity of circulation (though he does not use those terms)— ". . . there is thus a tendency to spend the largest amount of money possible in the shortest time span. . . . " (p. 585)—a decidedly "monetarist" proposition! (In terms of the framework adopted in Chapter 1, an increase in the velocity of circulation of money is equivalent to a decline in the demand for money.)

6. For simplicity, consider a two-sector economy, and define the general price level (P) as a geometric average of the price levels in "agriculture" (P_a) and "industry" (P_i):

$$P = P_a^\alpha P_i^{1-\alpha}.$$

Taking natural logarithms and time-derivatives, the rate of inflation will equal

$$p = \alpha p^* + p_i$$

where in keeping with the notation adopted in Chapter 1, lower case letters denote rates of change, and $P^* = P_a/P_i$ is the relative price of the agricultural good. Since $p_i \geq 0$ by the assumption of downward price rigidity, $p^* > 0$ implies that p will be necessarily > 0. (Note that if continuous time is denoted by the variable t, for any variable x the derivative of $1 nx$ with respect to t will equal $\partial \ln x /\partial t = (\partial x /\partial t)/x$, which is the rate of change of x in continuous time.)

7. Also, an additional theoretical consideration is relevant in this context. If purchasing power parity holds, then the devaluation of the exchange rate, which is an important element in p_m, will itself be a result of domestic inflation, and therefore p_m will not contribute information additional to that already contained in m and y_r. On the purchasing power parity theory of exchange rates see Officer (1976).

CHAPTER 3

INFLATION IN A SMALL COUNTRY: A CASE STUDY OF BOLIVIA

Most economic problems are the result of ignoring the most fundamental of economic lessons. Henry Hazlitt reiterates this in the following terms: "The art of economics consists in looking not merely at the immediate but at the longer effects of any act or policy; it consists in tracing the consequences of that policy not merely for one group but for all groups" (1962, p. 12). The recent Bolivian hyperinflation is a particularly telling illustruation of the effects of ignoring the long run.

Hyperinflation, defined by Cagan as a rate of monthly inflation of 50% or more, is a rare phenomenon. Apart from the recent Bolivian experience, there are only eight other cases on record in the whole of known monetary history, and even the Bolivian case qualified as a bona fide hyperinflation only during the first half of 1985. Bolivia is moreover sui generis in that it has the dubious distinction of being the only country that has achieved hyperinflation in peacetime, whereas all other known cases have occurred either in the midst of a military conflict, or in the aftermath of military defeat.

Viewed in perspective, however, there is nothing surprising about the recent Bolivian experience. In fact, the Bolivian story amounts almost to a textbook case of how short-sighted monetary policy and political instability can combine to destroy an economy, though it is easy to lose a longer run perspective in analyzing the Bolivian data, since the often dramatic developments of the early 1980s—three, four, and five digit inflation; the external debt crisis that erupted in 1981, culminating in suspension of payments in May 1984; growing social and labor unrest; political turmoil before, during, and after the government of the left-wing coalition led by Dr. Hernán Siles Zuazo—all these recent developments tend to eclipse the events and policies of the relatively quiet decade of the 1970s, which is accorded a much smaller share of analysts' attention, when it is not overlooked altogether. However, an informed analysis of the evolution of certain indicators during those years clearly shows that all of the turbulent developments of recent years were the inevitable outcome of certain trends initiated during the "quiet years," and the direct result of the failure of successive governments of different ideological stripes to take corrective action. It goes without saying that the reluctance of governments to make tough but necessary decisions, and their stubborn, persistent "live for today" attitudes, postponed the day of reckoning only by aggravating the situation, until the overdelayed but unavoidable adjustment took on the proportions of a catastrophe.

BACKGROUND: THE BOLIVIAN ECONOMY, 1972–78

Specifically, the Bolivian crisis was in a very basic sense the result of a narrowly conceived monetary policy, which had been traditionally identified almost exclusively with the maintenance of the exchange rate of the peso vis-à-vis the U.S. dollar. In effect, in Bolivia, as in many other Latin American countries, a stable exchange rate has long been considered the main, if not the only, standard of success in economic policy, while devaluation has been regarded as evidence and explicit recognition of failure. Historically, successive devaluations of the peso have always been traumatic, amounting sometimes to nothing short of a national drama, for which reason they have been avoided whenever possible. Even when this step has been reluctantly taken they have generally been insufficient compared to the magnitude of the adjustment required by the circumstances. The official exchange rate of the peso has thus had a chronic tendency to become overvalued with respect to the U.S. dollar, and exchange rate stability during the 1970s is therefore a highly misleading indicator of the inflationary pressures that were building up.

That decade, like most of Bolivia's monetary history, was a period of inflation. As is shown in Table 3.1, between 1972 and 1979 the money supply (M_1) increased by a factor of 4.7, as a result of which the internal price level (as measured by the CPI) also increased significantly, approximately by a factor of 3.8 (see Table 3.2). Since the exchange rate of the peso had been fixed at 20 pesos per U.S. dollar since 1972, this internal inflation implied that the peso was becoming increasingly overvalued. Indeed, by 1977 this was quite evident, since the peso was buying the same amount of dollars as in 1972, even though its internal purchasing power had declined by over 50%. This situation had to induce serious doubts as to the government's future ability to indefinitely maintain the exchange rate. Perhaps more importantly, the combination of internal inflation and a fixed exchange rate led to a steadily deteriorating external situation by inducing the continuous growth of imports, due to the widening gap between internal prices and the cost of imports, while export activity by the same token was gradually discouraged.[1]

This is clearly borne out by an examination of the balance of payments

Table 3.1
Bolivia: Monetary and Banking Statistics
(year-end, millions of pesos)

			1975 Pesos	
	Money Supply	Bank Deposits	Real Money Supply	Real Bank Deposits
1972	2,210	1,157	4,333	2,268
1973	2,969	1,509	4,303	2,186
1974	4,257	2,406	4,434	2,506
1975	4,759	3,105	4,665	3,044
1976	6,497	5,001	6,072	4,674
1977	7,855	6,384	6,600	5,365
1978	8,831	6,527	6,590	4,870
1979	10,304	6,510	5,257	3,321
1980	14,694	10,527	6,072	4,350
1981	17,587	14,925	5,804	4,926
1982	57,827	56,056	4,806	4,659
1983	177,500	137,200	3,440	2,658
1984	3,370,100	1,106,200	2,870	942
1985	207,000,000	83,000,000	2,136	856

Note: Money supply defined as currency outside banks plus demand deposits in banks (M_1). Bank deposits are the sum of demand plus savings and term deposits in banks. Real magnitudes are obtained by deflating the nominal magnitudes by the corresponding (year-end) values of the CPI reported in Table 3.2.

Source: *International Financial Statistics*, Yearbooks 1984, 1985, 1986.

(Table 3.3). In effect, already markedly in deficit by 1975-77, it deteriorated still further during and after 1978. In the five years from 1974 to 1979 legal imports more than doubled, while exports only increased 36% (even this small increase is misleading since it was due solely to the rather fortuitous fact that the prices of the country's principal mineral exports increased 80%, on average, during that period—in physical terms the volume of exports actually declined 30% over the same period).

The special circumstances of the Bolivian economy call for some explanatory comments on the balance of payments data. Note that traditionally exports have exceeded imports, with the exception of the years 1978 and 1979, in itself a clear indication of the degree of deterioration. In comparing exports and imports, however, the following facts should be borne in mind:

Table 3.2
Course of Inflation in Bolivia, 1972–86

	Consumer Price Index (1975 = 1)	Exchange Rate ($b/$us)	
		Official	Parallel
Dec 1972	0.51	20.00	–
Dec 1973	0.69	20.00	–
Dec 1974	0.96	20.00	–
Dec 1975	1.02	20.00	–
Dec 1976	1.07	20.00	–
Dec 1977	1.19	20.00	–
Dec 1978	1.34	20.00	–
Dec 1979	1.96	25.00	–
Dec 1980	2.42	25.00	–
Dec 1981	3.03	25.00	–
1982 Mar	3.90	44.00	48.20
June	4.79	101.70(n)	103.10
Sept	8.20	229.20(n)	256.90
Dec	12.03	200.00	283.00
1983 Mar	14.9	200.00	457
June	18.2	200.00	431
Sept	29.4	200.00	761
Dec	51.6	500.00	1,244
1984 Mar	84.1	500	2,800
June	209.9	2,000	3,250
Sept	348.6	5,000	14,600
Dec	1174.0	9,000	22,100
1985 Jan	1980	9,000	60,100
Feb	5602	50,000	120,000
Mar	7000	50,000	121,000
Apr	7826	50,000	156,600
May	10616	75,000	248,500
June	18948	75,000	448,000
July	31515	75,000	801,000
Aug	52460	75,000	1,050,000
Sept	82090	–	1,100,000
Oct	80297	–	1,100,000
Nov	82868	–	1,200,000
Dec	96866	–	1,600,000
1986 Jan	128840	–	2,100,000
Feb	137344	–	1,850,000
Mar	139915	–	1,950,000
Apr	144969	–	1,900,000
May	n.a.	–	1,900,000
June	n.a.	–	1,900,000

Note: During the period of the official "floating" peso, a part of export proceeds had to be sold to the monetary authorities at the official exchange rate of $b 44.00. This exchange regime lasted from April to October 1982.

Sources: *Consumer Prices. International Financial Statistics*, "Supplement on Price Statistics," Supplement Series No. 2, 1981; Banco Central de Bolivia, *Boletin Estadistico*, No. 253 (La Paz, Bolivia: Dec 1984), and *International Financial Statistics*, monthly issues, 1986.

Exchange Rate. Author's own records.

Table 3.3
Bolivia: Balance of Payments, 1974–84 ($U.S. millions)

	1974	1975	1976	1977	1978	1979	1980	1981	1982	1983	1984
Exports, FOB	556.5	444.7	563.0	634.3	627.3	761.8	941.9	909.1	827.7	755.1	724.4
Imports, FOB	-324.1	-469.9	-512.3	-579.0	-723.0	-815.0	-680.1	-680.1	-428.7	-473.1	-412.5
Services & Others (Net)	-109.0	-118.1	-118.2	-188.2	-261.9	-356.6	-436.0	-554.6	-537.0	-538.0	-578.4
CURRENT ACCOUNT	123.4	-143.3	-67.5	-132.9	-358.5	-409.8	-174.2	-325.6	-138.0	-256.0	-266.5
Errors	-77.6	-47.4	-63.4	-79.0	-84.7	-28.0	-260.2	-329.0	-50.6	80.4	-6.8
	45.8	-191.0	-130.9	-211.9	-443.2	-437.8	-434.4	-654.6	-188.6	-175.6	-273.3
CAPITAL ACCOUNT (Net)	-173.1	224.4	83.8	136.1	524.3	412.4	571.4	632.9	151.4	153.4	41.2
Change in Reserves	-127.3	33.4	-47.1	-75.8	81.1	-25.4	137.0	-21.7	-37.2	-22.2	-232.1

Source: International Financial Statistics, Yearbook 1986.

1. Imports are expressed FOB, that is, excluding transportation and insurance charges, which are consigned to the "services" account. Given its landlocked geography, in Bolivia these costs have always represented a large share of import costs. Therefore, the balance on "current account" is more meaningful than the simple "trade balance" (exports minus imports), since it includes the net effect of all other factors except capital movements.

2. It is well known that smuggling and contraband are an important element in Bolivia's international transactions, though by their very nature they are not reflected directly in the official trade figures. A rough idea of the movement in "net" smuggling is given by the movement in the "errors and omissions" account, which in most countries is a small element in the total balance of payments. In Bolivia it is an inordinately large item (sometimes exceeding in magnitude the balance on current account). Presumably, the "errors" largely reflect net illegal merchandise trade, but it probably includes some capital movements also. To separate these items is obviously impossible, nor can it be assumed that the "error" has been determined precisely, so to speak, since it is statistically computed as the net discrepancy between the current account, the capital account, and the change in international reserves, all of which contain their own errors of unknown magnitude.

Given these problems, no single figure of the balance of payments can be accepted uncritically, but even so, taken jointly the evolution of the different balances yields a clear vision of the deteriorating situation, and the sum of the current account and the error account gives a fair idea of the Bolivian economy's increasing external financing needs. In practice, the larger share of this financing took the form of public external debt. Indeed, most of this debt was not being used to finance investments, but solely for balance of payments financing. The rapid increase in the Bolivian government's foreign debt during the 1970s (see Table 3.4) is cold testimony to the effects of the exchange rate policy adopted. The correlation between the balance of payments and the growth of the public debt is quite clear, though it is certainly not perfect, since part of the external financing was in the form of private debt. Also, a part of the public debt originated in private debts guaranteed by the Bolivian government, which only later on became "public."[2]

In any case, it is quite clear that one of the key factors in the growth of the external debt was the situation of external disequilibrium created by the overvaluation of the peso, which was aggravated by the "flight" of private capital owing to growing doubts as to the government's ability to maintain the exchange rate indefinitely. (Thus, in a very basic sense the external public debt effectively financed a large share of the flight of private capital, and the burden implied by the service and eventual repayment of this debt amounts to a subsidy, financed by a tax on the Bolivian people at large, in favor of those who had the ability and foresight to accumulate assets abroad.)

This rapid growth in external debt in turn resulted in a high and rising service burden. The most frequently used measure of debt burden is the ratio of annual debt service to exports. Table 3.4 shows that the service of Bolivia's external public debt, which prior to 1971 never represented more than 11% of the value of exports, represented from 12 to 17% of annual exports between 1971 and 1976, in itself a significant deterioration, and was never less than 22% of exports after 1976. (This indicator actually underestimates the gravity of the situation, since exports were still highly dependent upon tin, which has always been subject to wide price fluctuations, and, as we have noted above, the volume of exports had been declining steadily, which had been compensated by an increase in export unit values. Even a small price decline would have had a strong adverse effect given the increasing debt service burden. Obviously, the fixed exchange rate could not stimulate the expansion of nontraditional exports.) Relevant in this regard is the change in the structure of the external public debt, particularly the relative increase in the debt to private banks, which is characterized by shorter terms, higher financial cost, and greater sensitivity to changes in interest rates in the world money market.

By 1977–78 it was evident, then, that the Bolivian economy required, at the very least, a fundamental exchange rate adjustment. However, the political chaos that befell the country in the period 1978–82, and the impolitical nature of the type of policy measures that the situation demanded, guaranteed the virtual impossibility of their adoption. In a situation that required realism in the economic sphere, Bolivia was confronted for three years with a sequence of transition governments, the kind of government least qualified, politically, for facing the country's fundamental problems.

MORE BACKGROUND: RECENT POLITICAL HISTORY

Modern Bolivian political history[3] dates from the aftermath of the Chaco War with Paraguay (1932–35), a long and costly disaster for Bolivia. In retrospect, the most important political result of that conflict was the establishment of rival socialist and radical political parties by many of the frustrated younger literate veterans—the so-called "Chaco generation"—directly challenging the traditional political system.

The initial result of this challenge was the overthrow, in 1936, of the civilian government by young military officers led by Col. David Toro and

Table 3.4
Bolivia: External Public Debt, 1971–83 ($U.S. millions)

	Disbursed Only	Total	Including Undisbursed Portions		Private Finance		Debt Service to Exports (%)
			Official Bilateral	Multilateral	Banks	Other	
31.12.1971	534.6	616.3	309.8	79.1	8.1	219.1	12.2
31.12.1972	628.1	763.6	376.5	89.2	35.2	262.7	17.9
31.12.1973	639.0	770.5	382.7	100.2	40.9	246.7	15.2
31.12.1974	708.4	894.6	445.2	138.8	91.9	218.7	11.0
31.12.1975	779.9	1202.7	534.8	269.9	164.2	233.8	14.4
31.12.1976	1000.1	1576.3	563.0	398.3	360.9	254.0	17.0
31.12.1977	1361.1	1962.6	693.1	466.7	575.5	227.3	22.5
31.12.1978	1665.5	2377.3	793.1	621.2	726.2	236.9	50.5(n)
31.12.1979	1834.9	2759.0	908.4	770.6	857.3	222.7	31.4
31.12.1980	2124.0	n.a.	n.a.	n.a.	n.a.	n.a.	27.2
31.12.1981	2421.9	3009.6	953.6	882.0	1005.5	168.6	26.2
31.12.1982	2555.5	3158.1	n.a.	n.a.	n.a.	n.a.	28.2
31.12.1983	2968.9	3849.0	n.a.	n.a.	n.a.	n.a.	30.5

Note: Service ratio is strongly influenced by pre-payments in this year.

n.a. = not available

Source: World Bank, *Annual Reports, 1972–85.*

Maj. Germán Busch, the first military government since 1880. "Military socialism" actually accomplished very little, besides nationalization of foreign oil concessions, though it did create an important and socially advanced labor legislation that was to have important effects in later years.

During the 1940s the numerous and diverse political groups began to coalesce into major national parties, of which the two most important were the Movimiento Nacionalista Revolucionario (MNR), and Marxist pro-Soviet Partido de la Izquierda Revolucionaria (PIR). In 1943 a civilian government was deposed by a military group that allied itself with the MNR. Headed by Col. Gualberto Villaroel, this allegedly profascist government was opposed by both right and left. In 1946 it was overthrown in a bloody revolution, and Villaroel was hanged from a lamppost in front of the presidential palace in Murillo Square.

The PIR thereafter attempted to rule in alliance with the older, more traditional parties (known collectively as "la rosca"), but this bizarre coalition, sarcastically dubbed "roscopirismo," predictably failed, and the PIR eventually dissolved and disappeared from the political scene. Meanwhile the MNR, recovering from its disaster under Villaroel, dissociated itself from its fascist wing and worked out an alliance with the PRIN, a small socialist party that nonetheless had a very strong following by the mineworkers, led by Juan Lechín.

The conservative parties proved unable to control the political tidal wave that had been building up ever since the Chaco defeat, and after the MNR won the presidential elections of 1951 the military intervened and formed a junta. After several unsuccessful but increasingly violent revolts, the MNR finally overthrew the military government in April 1952.

Thus began the Bolivian National Revolution. Under the leadership of Victor Paz Estensoro, head of the MNR, the new regime nationalized the mining concerns of the three biggest "tin barons"—Antenor Patiño, Carlos Víctor Aramayo, and Mauricio Hochschild—in October 1952. In August 1953 it decreed one of the most far-reaching land reforms ever enacted in Latin America. Politically, universal suffrage was granted with the abolition of literacy requirements for the vote.

Paz Estensoro was succeeded in 1956 by the (at the time) more conservative Hernán Siles Zuazo, whose main objective was to stop the runaway inflation that followed the excesses of the 1952 revolution. With economic support from the United States the inflation was brought under control, but most of the social spending programs were suspended as well. This resulted in a cleavage in party unity, alienating its leftwing, and particularly Lechín and his tin miners, the erstwhile backbone of the MNR, who were alienated still further when the government ended worker comanagement of the nationalized mines. (This estrangement between Siles and Lechín was a lasting one, and was destined to have tremendously important consequences for the next round of Bolivian inflation, 25 years later.)

Before this break of party unity, a "schedule" had been worked out between the leaders of the MNR. Paz Estensoro, Siles Zuazo, Walter Guevara Arce, and Juan Lechín would succeed to the presidency in that order. When Siles's term ended, however, the MNR renominated Paz Estensoro for a second term instead of choosing Guevara Arce, who thereby broke away from the party and formed his own Partido Revolucionario Auténtico (PRA).

The split during the 1964 election was much more damaging. Lechín was denied the MNR nomination, and Paz Estensoro was again renominated. Lechín then broke away to form still another party, and at the same time Siles Zuazo himself broke with the MNR, forming his own Movimiento Nacionalista Revolucionario de Izquierda (MNRI). Although Paz Estensoro was elected for a third term, he served only a few months before being overthrown by his own vice-president, Gen. René Barrientos Ortuño, who seized power with the support of most of the civilian opposition (including dissident factions of the MNR), and of the military, which until then had been keeping a low political profile.

From 1964 until his death in a helicopter accident in 1969, Barrientos consolidated the reforms of the National Revolution, demobilizing, however, the popular groups that had arisen to power during its course. (It was also during the Barrientos regime that a poorly organized guerrilla campaign led by the Cuban-Argentinian revolutionary "Che" Guevara was destroyed, in 1967.)

Barrientos's death brought into office his vice-president, Luis A. Siles Salinas, who was forcibly removed in mid-1969 by Gen. Alfredo Ovando Candia. After he had nationalized the holdings of the Gulf Oil Company, Candia himself was forced out in October 1970 by a more radical general, Juan José Torres.

Torres's military backing was precarious, and he therefore sought civilian backing from the left. A "Popular Assembly" was established, composed predominantly of labor union leaders, plus assorted delegates from the left-wing political parties. Many viewed it as an incipient "Soviet."

In August 1971 Torres was overthrown in a bloody coup d'état led by Col. Hugo Banzer Suarez, who remained in power for seven years. During his first two years Banzer had the support of the faction of the MNR led by Paz Estensoro, as well as that of the MNR's traditional enemy, the Falange Socialista Boliviana, a right-wing party with an enigmatic name. During most of its time in power, however, the Banzer government was a strict military dictatorship.

By 1978 the regime of political stability that Gen. Banzer had forged was subject to strong pressures for a "democratización." After 14 years of "extra-constitutional" governments, the popular clamor for democracy was overwhelming, and a civil resistance movement backed by the Catholic Church eventually forced Banzer to call elections. (It should be mentioned that international pressures also contributed to the "democratization.")

The first attempt at democracy was not very encouraging in its results. The official returns of the July 1978 election favored the "banzerista" candidate, Juan Pereda Asbún, but the results were challenged, and finally, toward the end of July, Pereda simply seized power in a bloodless coup, promising new elections within six months, which he later postponed to May 1980.

Pereda was deposed in November 1978 by Gen. David Padilla, who promised elections for July 1979, and made good on his promise. The results of this second round of elections were inconclusive. No candidate achieved a majority, so election of the president had to be decided in secondary elections in the Congress. Given the country's political polarization, which was clearly reflected in the composition of the Congress, no agreement could be achieved, and the result was a political compromise in which Walter Guevara Arce, the president of the Senate, was named "interim president" of the republic for one year, with a mandate to call and preside over still another general election in May 1980.

Guevara was not to fulfill his mandate, however, since he was overthrown in November 1979 by a Col. Alberto Natusch. Symptomatic of the degree of polarization of power that had taken place in Bolivia is the fact that Natusch did not manage to consolidate his putsch, in spite of the use of brutal acts of repression.[4]

After a confusing two-week period, Congress appointed Lidia Gueiler, then president of the Chamber of Deputies, to finish the mandate originally accorded to Guevara. She thus presided over the elections of May 1980, which were also indecisive. This time, however, the left-wing coalition headed by Hernán Siles Zuazo obtained a marginal lead in Congress. But before Congress could carry out its decision to elect Siles, who had in fact obtained a relative majority of the popular vote, still another military coup brought Gen. Luis García Meza to power the following month.

With the García Meza regime began perhaps the most disgraceful period of modern Bolivian history. The new government was accused by the international press of abetting the cocaine traffic, even that the coup had been financed by the drug mafia. García Meza was eventually deposed in a palace coup, replaced by Gen. Celso Torrelio in August 1981, who in turn handed over the government a year later to Gen. Guido Vildoso, of short duration. Vildoso finally called the 1980 Congress back into session, whereupon it elected Hernán Siles who assumed power in October 1982.

THE FATEFUL YEAR, 1982

In the midst of this sometimes comic, too often tragic musical chair alternation of elections and military takeovers, economic pressures were building up a momentum of their own. By their very nature, of course, none of the officially designated "transition" governments was qualified for taking the needed economic adjustment measures. But the García Meza regime, ostensibly of indefinite duration, was not inclined to do so either. Between 1978 and 1981 successive Bolivian governments allowed the process to follow its own logic. (The Gueiler government did in fact devalue the peso in December 1979, from 20 to 25 pesos per U.S. dollar, but by then this was really no more than a symbolic act, well below the magnitude of the adjustment required by the circumstances.)

The overvaluation of the peso could only be maintained via increasing external debt. This was indeed the main cause of this indebtedness. Any country's debt capacity, however, has a limit, and the increasing debt service burden suggested that by 1981 Bolivia had already reached this limit. Nevertheless, up to the very last moment the authorities continued to sell U.S. dollars at the official exchange rate, even after the foreign exchange reserves had been depleted altogether. In August 1981 the crisis was triggered by an almost inconceivable event: A check drawn by the Banco Central de Bolivia against a New York bank was returned due to insufficient funds.

In that month of August the new Torrelio government established a system of foreign exchange controls. The new system was actually quite superfluous—there was no foreign exchange to allocate. An impasse of several months ensued in which the foreign exchange applications accumulated, allocations were minimal, and the official exchange rate remained "fixed" at 25 pesos. Meanwhile, in the street the "parallel" rate gradually rose, and by December 1981 the dollar had reached more or less 50 pesos.

In February 1982 the government devalued the official exchange rate to 44 pesos, but again the move was purely symbolic, since there were no "official" dollars to sell even at the new rate. Since the central bank lacked the wherewithal to support the official exchange rate, it had to openly recognize the situation sooner or later. This occurred the next month, in March 1982, when the floating of the peso was decreed.[5] Actually, the new regime was a "dual" exchange rate system, with a free market and an official market that still operated with the fixed rate of 44 pesos. Practically all imports were purchased at the free rate, while exporters were forced to sell 40% of their foreign exchange proceeds at the official rate (which the government apparently used to service its debt, since allocations of foreign exchange at the official rate were minimal), and could only sell 60% of their proceeds at the free rate. As the free rate gradually rose, the gap between the cost of imports and the weighted average exchange rate that exporters received widened more and more. Clearly, this could not encourage export activity, the ultimate source of foreign exchange supply, and the free market exchange rate rose higher and higher through the months. By September-October, a half-year of floating had driven the free market dollar above the 200 peso mark, to which Bolivians attached much symbolic value (before this happened it was said that if the dollar passed 200, nothing would stop it).

The critical year for the Bolivian economy was 1982. The political changes occurring later that year were to have an important impact upon the course of the inflation, as will be shown below, but in the meantime the sudden increase in the cost of imports (a 300% devaluation in 9-10 months) was having two important effects:

The balance of payments data show that legal imports declined (in dollar terms) by about 40% (the effect on illegal trade, to judge from the errors account, was even more dramatic). This had a highly adverse impact on economic activity, since the Bolivian economy after a decade of overvalued exchange rates had come to depend upon imports even for the most basic inputs. That year the real GDP declined by almost 7%. This had a direct effect upon prices but its fiscal effects were much more important in contributing to the acceleration of the inflationary process.

This decline in real GDP had to cause perforce a more or less proportional decline in fiscal revenues. However, the Bolivian tax system—notoriously inefficient, obsolete, and corrupt—guaranteed even more fatal fiscal and monetary effects from these developments. Traditionally, fiscal revenues in Bolivia have depended to a large extent upon customs revenues, which of course depend upon the volume of legal imports. These declined significantly in 1982, as we have seen. Moreover, inflation reduced the real value of customs revenues even further, since they were appraised and collected at the overvalued official exchange rate of 44 pesos per dollar. The real value of internal revenues was affected by another very common problem in inflationary economies: typically, these taxes are collected with a lag, and therefore current tax revenues are based on incomes of earlier periods. When inflation is relatively high, the time lag between a tax's accrual and its actual collection causes a decline in the real value of fiscal revenues. Due to these factors, in 1982 the Bolivian government's fiscal revenues declined by almost 50% in real terms. Therefore, even if the government had only maintained the level of public spending in real terms, the real fiscal deficit would have increased by 70%. (Due to the decline in real GDP, even a constant real deficit would have implied a heavier economic burden.) Clearly, the financing of this deficit had to cause a significant increase in the money supply, feeding the inflationary process. Expectations of future inflation, by now well entrenched, contributed to accelerate the process, due to the decline in real monetary balances in view of the high real cost of holding money. Prices, in effect, were rising faster than the money supply (that is, the money supply was declining in real terms), which in turn magnified the inflationary impact of successive money supply increases. The only way out would have been a drastic reform of the tax system, or a decline in real public expenditure. Under the circumstances both options were utopian.

Therefore, it is likely that Bolivia was by then well embarked upon a vicious circle of inflation generated by the monetary expansion required to finance increasing fiscal deficits induced by the inflation itself. (For an early formalization of this type of "self-sustaining" inflation see Olivera, 1967; see also Aghevli and Kahn, 1978.) However, though it is rather academic to speculate as to what the course of the inflation would have been had the government limited itself to maintaining the real level of public spending, it would probably have been much lower, and though the stage was set for continued deterioration in the absence of radical reforms in the fiscal field, the deterioration would also have been a slower and much more gradual process. More than any other factor, the Bolivian hyperinflation was set loose by the inordinate increase in public spending in 1982, which in real terms was two times higher than in 1981. This is clearly seen from Table 3.5, which shows that public expenditure (in millions of pesos) increased from 24,286 in 1981 to 130,275 in 1982. To be sure, part of this increase was due to inflation, but even adjusting the figures for the increase in the GDP deflator yields a twofold increase in real terms which, given the decline in real fiscal revenues, resulted in a fourfold increase in the real deficit that year. This increase in the deficit, the financing of which was the direct cause of the subsequent inflation, was due to a real increase in public spending that simply cannot be attributed to the effects of inflation itself.

A closer inspection of the fiscal data of 1982 shows that most of this increase in spending took place in the last quarter (see Table 3.6), coinciding with the accession to power of Dr. Siles's left-wing coalition.

These figures clearly show that in the last three months of 1982 public spending in nominal terms was over nine times greater than in the previous quarter, and even adjusting for inflation almost six times greater. The resulting increase in the fiscal deficit, and subsequent inflation, can hardly be attributed to inflation itself. In any country, even with a sound economy, a deficit of this order would have had a very strong inflationary impact. In the Bolivian situation, with a fragile tax system in which inflation magnified the deficit, and with an ever shrinking real GDP, the effect was to set off the worst inflationary crisis in its republican history: 330% in 1983, 2,300% in 1984, and an annual rate of 29,800% in the first eight months of 1985.

THE COURSE OF INFLATION, 1982–85

Statistics are fragmentary for 1983 and later years, though in a sense they are not really very necessary. "Hard" data would only serve to document

Table 3.5
Bolivia: Public Finance, 1974–84 (millions of pesos)

	Fiscal Revenues	Public Expenditure	GDP Deflator	1980 Pesos	
				Real Revenues	Real Expenditures
1977	7,641	10,954	53.7	14,229	20,398
1978	8,540	11,542	60.9	14,023	18,952
1979	8,384	15,035	72.0	11,644	20,882
1980	11,793	21,522	100.0	11,793	21,522
1981	14,069	24,286	127.8	11,009	19,003
1982	19,316	130,275	334.6	5,773	38,934
1983	46,988	356,287	1240.1	3,789	28,730
1984	556,122	4,857,351	18613.0	2,988	26,096

Sources: *Revenues and Expenditures.* Banco Central de Bolivia, *Boletín Estadístico*, No. 253 (La Paz, Dec 1984).

GDP Deflator. International Financial Statistics, Yearbook 1986, and *Statistical Yearbook for Latin America and the Caribbean* (Santiago, Chile: United Nations, 1986).

Table 3.6
Bolivia: Public Finance, 1982

Quarter	1	2	3	4
Revenues	2,470	4,723	4,051	8,071
Expenditure	6,381	7,015	11,945	104,934
CPI (1975 = 100)	354.1	458.7	696.2	1086.6
Real Revenues	697	1,029	582	743
Real Expenditure	1,801	1,529	1,442	9,656

Note: "Real" figures in terms of 1975 pesos. All monetary amounts in millions.

Source: International Financial Statistics, Nov 1983.

the inevitable outcome of the course the Bolivian economy had set upon in 1982. The stage was set for a process of self-sustained accelerating inflation.

The exchange rate is the best indicator of the course of the inflation (see Table 3.2). In November 1982 the new Siles government abolished the floating exchange rate, and devalued the official exchange rate to 200 pesos per U.S. dollar. In the parallel dollar market, illegal but more or less tolerated, the dollar continued its upward movement, slowly at first, but with sudden and unexpected leaps in the first few months of 1983. In February it jumped from 280 to 380 over one weekend. By June 1983 the "street" dollar was over 400 pesos, and continued its daily rise, with occasional declines. In November the official rate was again devalued, to 500, but the street rate was by then well over 1,000 pesos and rising, reaching 1,700 in January 1984, and bordering 3,000 by March. To all intents and purposes, the official exchange rate was simply following, with a lag, the rise of the street rate. In April 1984, the government once again devalued the official exchange rate, this time to 2,000 pesos. In 16 months the price of the official dollar had multiplied by a factor of 10.

The street dollar more or less stabilized, about an average value of roughly 3,500 pesos, for a relatively long period, from April 1984 to the end of July 1984, when it again began to rise quickly. By mid-August it fluctuated, within a rather wide band, around 9,000. That month the government established a so-called "multiple" exchange system, keeping the old rate of 2,000 for certain "preferential" operations, with another rate of 5,000 for most other "official" transactions, and even recognizing the parallel (street) exchange rate for certain types of operations. Meanwhile the street rate had again "stabilized" in September, fluctuating about 15,000 till mid-November when it once again began to rise, stopping briefly at about 19,000 for a few weeks (apparently due to a long series of banking sector strikes). By the end of December 1984 the monetary effect of a series of wage increases dictated in November, magnified by the year-end social benefits, drove the street rate to between 22,000 and 26,000 the last week of the year, and in the first week of 1985 it rose to over 50,000.

The official rate lagged miserably behind. Devalued to 9,000 as part of the November package, it was again devalued in February 1985 to 50,000, and later again in May to 75,000. By then events were unfolding so quickly that no fixed exchange rate could help but become outdated even before it was decreed. The process of preparing, agreeing upon, and passing a devaluation decree was so cumbersome that the new official rate was already far behind the street rate weeks before it became law.

The course of the exchange rate during 1985 can be summarized briefly: the street dollar fluctuated between 100,000 and 200,000 pesos between February and April; passing 200,000 in May; jumping then to over 400,000 in June; 800,000 in July; and passing the million peso mark by August, when the new government of Victor Paz Estensoro took office.

The public's attitude toward the dollar was ambivalent. There was a general notion that the dollar, "that accursed currency," was somehow to blame for the disaster. The dollar was the theme of numerous plays on words: sidewalk money changers dealt in "dolores" (pains), and the fluctuations of the exchange rate produced "dólares de cabeza" (a play on "dolores de cabeza"—headaches). On the other hand, people were realistic, and lacking alternative investment options, the dollar was the generalized form of saving—any momentary excess of liquidity was immediately "converted" to "real money." The real cost of holding pesos for very long was quite high even as of mid-1984. By 1985 it was prohibitive. The following extract from a front-page *Wall Street Journal* article (13 August 1985) is perhaps a trifle dramatized, but it is nonetheless an entirely accurate description of the situation:

> When Edgar Miranda gets his monthly teacher's pay of 25 million pesos, he hasn't a moment to lose. Every hour, pesos drop in value. So, while his wife rushes to market to lay in a month's supply of rice and noodles, he is off with the rest of the pesos to change them into black-market dollars. . . . It is easier to comprehend what happens to the 38-year-old Mr. Miranda's pay if he doesn't quickly change it into dollars. The day he was paid a dollar cost 500,000 pesos. So he received \$50. Just days later, with the rate at 900,000 pesos, he would have received \$27.

No one can ever know how many dollars people stored "under the matresses," but there must have been a great many since the occasional sharp drops in the dollar exchange rate would provoke as much (if not more) consternation as the more routinary increases.

Rises in the price of the dollar were invariably attributed to manipulation by the sidewalk money dealers, and each period of substantial rises would call forth "batidas" against this guild by the authorities. Lack of a formal market, and sporadic persecution of the currency dealers, hindered market efficiency. Any given day could witness a broad range of quotations from one dealer to another; the only beneficiaries appeared to be the dealers themselves.

Foreign visitors would derive much mock-horrified amusement from the tragicomic spectacle of thousands of people carrying their money about in string-tied bundles. A news report in a European journal in late 1984 informed that a man had paid for his dinner in a La Paz restaurant with just over one pound of money! By that time most bank vaults had overflowed—they could no longer hold the vast amounts of currency involved, and storage sacks were simply piled up in bank corridors and emptied offices for the duration. "Bill-counting" had become an occupation much in demand, but given the magnitude of the task, even at banks the job of "counting" small denomination bills was limited to "side-counting" the tied and closely packed bundles of currency—usually only the number of small packets of (presumably) ten bills that each bundle contained was actually counted. Given the practical difficulty of counting 25 million pesos in 10,000 peso notes (worth about $ U.S. 50 in mid-June 1985), money received in payment had to be accepted with some degree of faith, which naturally incited not a few abuses.

Despite these difficulties, most transactions would be carried out in physical cash, and checks were used rarely, only in special types of payments. Outsiders might speculate that this was due to the rampant nature of the inflation, though the decline of the bank check had actually been noticeable for quite some time. The origin of this decline has more to do with the erosion of public confidence in the banking system as a result of a long series of bank strikes, unexpected "bank holidays" following each devaluation of the official exchange rate, and the fact that banks frequently would be forced to close their doors to the public due to a "lack of currency." This would never fail to mystify foreign visitors, since the crisis was so obviously due to an overabundance of currency, but the answer actually lies at the heart of the process.

Already by 1983 over 85% and at times up to 90% of government spending was financed by credit from the central bank, and book credits to treasury accounts were the major source of money creation. At times, however, these book credits exceeded the actual availability of physical cash at the central bank, since new notes were printed abroad (at great cost in scarce foreign currency. It was reported at one point that purchases of newly printed notes were costing $ U.S. 20 million per annum, making it the third largest single import item, after wheat and mining equipment.) Frequently, as checks drawn by the government were presented and cashed, the central bank would run out of notes, and resort to paying out of the reserves of the other banks (which were required by law to hold the bulk of their reserves on deposit with the central bank). Therefore, when the commercial banks needed to avail themselves of their reserves, the central bank not infrequently had to refuse, and the banks would then simply close till further notice. Understandably, checks were not a popular means of payment.

In this situation, issues of new, higher denomination notes were always welcome. The new notes would invariably command a premium in terms of the older, low denomination notes, which had to be carried in bundles. Currency dealers would typically quote the dollar at different rates, one for "big" money, and another for "peasant currency," as the lower denomination notes were called.

In retrospect the magnitude and frequency of the continuing devaluations of the peso seem hardly surprising, in view of the preceding analysis, but they were nonetheless alarming. Even more alarming than the devaluations themselves, however, was the abrupt and sudden manner in which inflation followed its course. The global analysis of trends over more or less long periods is actually rather misleading, since these trends give a false impression of relatively smooth and uniform movement. In fact, perhaps the most remarkable aspect of the course of inflation in the short run is that, far from being a series of smooth and continuous increases, it is rather characterized by long periods of relative stability, which are suddenly broken by sharp and unexpected semi-general increases, which are again followed by calm periods that induce the belief that the inflation has somehow "stopped," prelude to a new round of increases. (This pattern seems to characterize Latin American inflations generally, regardless of the level of inflation—see Appendix.) It is almost as if inflationary pressures accumulate in some manner, creating an unstable balance of forces—unstable in the sense that once some critical tension is reached, any small change can set off a sudden, catastrophic movement.

As in most inflationary episodes, inflation has not been an unmitigated disaster for everyone. Many businesses, especially those lucky enough to obtain peso-denominated loans, have profited handsomely. At the 200% yearly interest rates prevailing in January 1985, bank loans were little more than outright cash gifts. The majority of the people, needless to say, were not in this racket. For most people, survival lay in the underground economy, of which the cocaine traffic is the most notorious aspect, though vastly overrated. To be sure, an increasingly large number of Bolivians became involved in the *narco-trafico*, in one way or another, but certainly not a majority, not even a significant minority. On the other hand, almost every Bolivian had to survive by some sort of illegal or extralegal activity: Most public employees, at every level of public administration, supplemented their meager salaries by graft; smuggling has traditionally been a tolerated, even honored, occupation; thousands of people made a living by money changing, profiting from often sizeable price differentials in an imperfect market; speculation in scarce essentials, invariably subject to price controls, was rife, and black markets thrived in everything from powdered milk to gasoline; political connections, whether with government officials or with the powerful trade union leadership, were capital assets, helpful to obtain an extra 100-pound bag of sugar at the official price (always hard to get even at market prices), a license for a smuggled car, or even "official" dollars for a trip abroad. Moral values were eroding almost as quickly as monetary values. To quote again from the August 1985 *Wall Street Journal* article:

> Workers stage repeated strikes and steal from their bosses. The bosses smuggle production abroad, take out phony loans, duck taxes—anything to get dollars for speculation. Tin production at the state mines, for example, dropped to 12,000 tons last year from

18,000. The miners pad their wages by smuggling out the richest ore in their lunch pails, and the ore goes by a contraband network into neighboring Peru. Without a major tin mine, Peru now exports some 4,000 metric tons of tin a year.

Bolivians lived by their wits, but runaway inflation is a negative-sum game, and the struggle is eventually a losing one. Some ended better off, but most people were poorer after the event, and every indicator points to the fact that Bolivia as a whole, always a poor country, was even poorer in 1985 than it was in 1980. During the great inflation the middle classes gradually drew upon their savings from earlier, better years, and the country steadily depleted its stock of physical capital. Industrial machinery went without maintenance or repair, vehicles stopped rolling for lack of spare parts, wear and tear slowly eroded the entire fixed capital structure. Businesses had little incentive to invest in productive capacity, since cash flow was preferably directed to more liquid, speculative investments.

As of year-end 1986 no adequate GDP statistics were available even for 1984, much less for 1985, but every objective indicator points to a sharp decline in economic activity. This decline was due to at least three main factors, all directly related to the inflation and the attendant social unrest.

1. An immediate factor, as we have stressed above, was the abrupt decline in imports, including raw materials and inputs for domestic industry, due to the shortage of foreign exchange and its high and rising real cost.

2. The drop in exports, with its multiplier effect on real GDP, due to the policy of paying exporters at overvalued official exchange rates.

3. Labor unrest, particularly during 1984 and 1985, was both an effect as well as a cause of the drop in production and the resulting decline in real wages. In effect, though purely political factors no doubt played an important role in successive confrontations between the Siles government and the trade union movement (led by Siles's old enemy, Juan Lechín), growing labor disorder was ultimately motivated by the desire to minimize the reduction in the working classes' real standard of living, efforts which acquired an ever-increasing sense of urgency as inflation accelerated.

This situation, conflictive in itself, was aggravated by the confusing wages policy of the Siles government. In November 1982 the government committed itself to indexing the minimum wage to the CPI, but the system never worked, partly because the workers did not really trust the official CPI figures (at one point the CPI was reportedly "negotiated" between the government and the trade union federation). Successive wage decrees were never granted by the government, but literally extracted by the workers through recourse to strikes, which were also used increasingly as a political tool to oppose successive stabilization programs. Continuing inflation and sporadic general wage increases made for wide fluctuations in real wages, which highlighted social tensions, while the resulting labor actions depressed production still further. In this regard, it should be noted that in both 1984 and 1985, nationwide general strikes paralyzed the entire country for two whole months (April and November 1984, April and September 1985), in addition to local and sectoral strikes.

STABILIZATION EFFORTS

Since 1982, the Siles government attempted five stabilization programs, the so-called "paquetes económicos," adopted in November 1982, November 1983, April 1984, November 1984, and February 1985. All failed due to their ad hoc nature, excessive reliance on purely short-term adjustments, and the general lack of a sense of continuity. Usually, the "stabilization" measures were little more than ex post facto adjustments for inflation in wages, in the pricing of public utilities and energy, and in the official exchange rate. The latter were invariably insufficient —though the CPI increased over 380,000% between May 1981 and May 1985, the official exchange rate was readjusted only eight times over the same period, once in February 1982, in each of the aforementioned "packages," and two isolated adjustments in August 1984 and May 1985.

In the dynamics of the Bolivian inflationary process, the rigid exchange rate policy itself became one of the main sources of the public sector deficit. In effect, public sector revenues came to depend significantly upon the official exchange rate—the prices of state-produced oil products and electricity, for instance, were all linked to the official exchange rate, as were the revenues of the state-owned tin mines, and of course the revenues from import duties—while public sector expenditures increased with the general price level, which was highly correlated with the parallel exchange rate. Thus, the widening gap between the official and parallel exchange rates resulted in an essentially passive monetary policy, in which the central bank merely issued the ever-increasing amounts of new money required to finance the growing public sector deficit.

By the end of 1984 the country was bordering on total anarchy. Strikes were no longer the only form of pressure used by the workers to force their demands. Increasingly, recourse was had to street demonstrations, road blocking, physical occupation of public offices and industrial installations, and kidnapping of employers and even of high public officials.

Overwhelmed by the reigning disorder, and no doubt with an eye to the very real possibility of a military takeover that would effectively put an end to the democratic experiment he was presiding, Dr. Siles decided in January 1985 to cut short his own presidential mandate by one year, calling for new general elections to be held in June 1985.

The 1985 elections were essentially a contest between the Acción Democrática Nacionalista (ADN), the right-wing party of former dictator Hugo Banzer, and the faction of the old MNR headed by Victor Paz Estensoro. Even if the left were not divided into 20 or so parties, many with their own squabbling splinter factions, the economic fiasco of the Siles government had produced widespread disenchantment with left-leaning politicians. Banzer in fact obtained a slight lead in the popular vote, with Paz a close second, but, as in previous elections, no candidate obtained an absolute majority, and Paz was finally elected in secondary elections in the Congress, with the support of the left-wing groups.

Paz Estensoro assumed his fourth presidential term on 6 August 1985, and three weeks later, on 29 August, he surprised even many of his closest supporters by launching Supreme Decree No. 21060, which generally became known as the New Economic Policy (NEP). The main target of the NEP was the inflation, but this was not just another "paquete económico." This time the government was determined not merely to adjust for past inflation, but to stop the process by attacking its root source in the bloated public sector deficit.

Thus the fixed official exchange rate was simply abolished, as were all food subsidies, and the prices of gasoline and related oil products were increased sixfold to world market levels. The NEP in fact abolished all price controls, and virtually all import and export restrictions.

In addition, the wage and salaries legislation—which over the years had evolved into a Byzantine web of laws and regulations pertaining to bonuses, benefits, subsidies, severance pay, etc.—was simplified, and the Bolivian banking system was freed of scores of restrictions.

Since a large share of the public sector deficit originated in state-owned enterprises, the NEP contemplated radical changes in the status of these companies (which is rather ironic, since many of them were established during Dr. Paz's first presidency, in 1952–56). For instance, the plan called for the decentralization of COMIBOL, the giant state mining concern, as well as that of YPFB, the state oil company.

A more drastic fate befell the Corporación Boliviana de Fomento (CBF), a holding company of state-owned agroindustrial enterprises. CBF was dissolved outright, its 24 companies transferred to the autonomous development corporations of the provinces where they operate. According to the plan, the central government was to have nothing to do with them in the future.

Finally, in the most controversial measure of all, public sector wages were frozen until 31 December, 1985.

To say that the country was stunned is to understate matters. The morning after the decree was sheer chaos. In what appeared to be one last drunken spurt, inflation went out with a bang. The price of everything surged by about 100%, though the dollar fell crazily from about 1.5 million pesos before the announcement to 1.2 million the day after, and to 1 million pesos over the first weekend (where it more or less stabilized during the month of September.) In the heat of the confusion, many shopkeepers justified their prices by saying that "Even the dollar is worthless now." The next few days, however, prices began to fall back again, in spite of a nationwide labor strike, and by mid-September most consumer goods were even somewhat cheaper than before the decree.

The negative reaction of left-leaning forces to the NEP was to be expected, but less expected was the initial reaction of Banzer's ADN, the major right-wing party. Some ADN spokesmen went so far as to describe the NEP as "treasonous," but much of this was probably pique at being "outrighted" by Dr. Paz, the wily grand old man of Bolivian politics. Indeed, most of the business sector, Banzer's major constituency, came out flatly in favor of the NEP, and the ADN may well be the major long-run political casualty of the change in policy. (As one wit put it, having stolen the election from Banzer with the help of the left, Paz had then stolen his program, and even his constituency.)

Consequently, the weeks following the NEP decree were politically stormy—in Congress and in the streets. Juan Lechín, the leader of the national trade union federation (COB), called for a national labor strike, a tactic he had used successfully to thwart every major policy initiative of the previous government. This time, however, response to the strike call was weak from the start, and Lechín's "cobistas" lost ground with each passing day. The government was in fact initially able to maintain order with little overt repression, for instance, mass demonstrations were thwarted by the simple expedient of denying the unions the use of official government vehicles.

By the end of the second week the COB held its ground only in the traditionally combative mining sector, and in air and railway transport. Finally, the government invoked a constitutional prerogative, decreeing an emergency state of siege, and arrested several hundred labor leaders, which effectively put an end to the strike. Most of the arrested labor leaders were released shortly after the government obtained from Congress an extension of the state of siege, which passed as a result of what was described as an "historic accord" between the MNR and ADN. A pleasant note, considering Bolivia's turbulent history, is that this latest bout of turmoil did not claim a single fatality.

AFTERMATH

By mid-1986 it was quite clear that the NEP had effectively stopped the inflation, but in retrospect it is difficult to determine exactly when this occurred. In effect, though prices stopped in their tracks during the first three months after the decree, in which period the rate of inflation dropped to practically zero (at least according to the official CPI), they began to rise again in December, showing a mild but sustained upward trend till February 1986, when they again appear to have stabilized. As of year-end 1986 no official data were available for the CPI beyond April 1986, but the trend in the exchange rate suggests that the inflation had definitely ended by mid-1986. It too had risen sharply in December, and by January 1986 it stood at 2 million pesos. Since then it has fluctuated somewhat, but by year-end it was still in that vicinity.

The tenacity with which Dr. Paz has adhered to the NEP in spite of its unpopularity is remarkable in itself, but what is perhaps even more remarkable is that he has managed so far to stick to the program in spite of dramatically unfavorable developments in the world tin market. In effect, the international price of tin literally collapsed in the last week of October 1986, when the NEP was not yet two months old. This is bound to have serious long-run effects on the Bolivian economy, since most of the state-owned mines were already unprofitable even before the price collapse, and the government now seems determined to close them if necessary. From the point of view of the NEP, of course, the timing of the tin market crash could not have been worse, and the resulting uncertainty as to the government's determination to carry on with the stabilization probably explains the brief resurgence of inflation toward the end of 1985. Also, the uncertain future of thousands of miners has aggravated the hardships associated with the wage freeze. Protests, demonstrations, and general strikes characterized 1986 just as much as they did the previous two years. In August 1986, a year after the NEP decree, miners staged a mass march on La Paz to protest the projected closure of mines. The marchers had to be forcibly turned back by army units, and Paz's government had to resort again to declaring a state of siege. Bolivia is facing a rude awakening on coming out of the nightmare.

Meanwhile the great Bolivian inflation is dead and gone. Perhaps the most fitting epitaph is the following item reported in the Bolivian newspaper *El Mundo* (Santa Cruz, 14 Nov 1985):

The Central Bank will construct special ovens to burn banknotes in disuse that are now stored in rented warehouses. Jaime Escobar, a director of the Central Bank, reported that thousands of tons of notes are out of circulation. He added that several forms of disposing of these notes were studied, but he pointed out that they cannot be processed into cardboard or other materials due to their chemical composition. He explained that the idea of selling the notes to the paper industry has been therefore discarded, . . . "They are all the previous denominations, such as $b. 1, 5, 50, 100, 500, 1000, 5000, and 10000, which due to hyperinflation are out of circulation. . . . Renting the immense warehouses where this money is stored is a big expense which we have to cut," said Jaime Escobar. He also noted that the incineration of these notes will require special ovens, though he did not say how much they would cost, and that the magnitude of the notes in disuse is such that their total incineration will take about six months.

NOTES

1. Quite apart from the external disequilibrium that the overvaluation of the peso was causing, it was also stimulating inflation directly. Costs of production in the exporting sector (mainly mining) increased directly with the internal inflation, although revenues in pesos were fixed with the exchange rate, increasing only with an increase in world minerals prices, beyond the control of the local producer. Consequently, the increasing operating deficits of the state-owned mines contributed to the overall public sector deficit, which had to be financed with currency issues. The policy of maintaining the fixed exchange rate in spite of internal inflation was equivalent to a subsidy in favor of the commercial-importing sector, a subsidy that was paid in the first instance by the mining-exporting sector, and ultimately by the people at large.

2. The ambitious development projects initiated by the Banzer government, which called for enormous public investments (financed in part by external debt, and partly by internal debts, that is, currency issues) that later proved to be non-productive, have been justly criticized. It is only fair to note, however, that the private sector has had its own share of white elephants financed externally with guarantees of the Bolivian government. In the Santa Cruz area alone there are the cases of the installation of an entirely superfluous sugar mill; a totally overdimensioned textile complex that has to import raw material to supplement the insufficient cotton that Bolivia produces; and no less than three vegetable oil factories when one is more than sufficient to supply the Bolivian market. The list can go on ad nauseam. Political-economic discourse in Bolivia has introduced two new verbs to the language: in response to rumors that the new leftist government headed by Dr. Siles was programming a series of nationalizations, critics accused the government of attempting to "comibolize" the economy, in allusion to the grossly inefficient Corporación Minera de Bolivia (COMIBOL), which administrates the mines nationalized in 1952. Government supporters replied that previous regimes had "sheratonized" the economy, referring to the policy of financing fastuous but failed private sector projects, such as the La Paz Sheraton Hotel, with external debts guaranteed by the Bolivian government.

3. One of the best surveys of modern Bolivian social and political history is that by Klein (1982). The volume edited by Ladman (1982) also contains several informative papers. On recent political developments see Queiser Morales (1980), Mitchell (1981), and Alexander (1985).

4. At that time, this author had occasion to transact some business at a Bolivian consulate abroad. When I asked the consul about recent political-military events in Bolivia, he replied laconically: "You tell me who is president in Bolivia."

5. Bolivians, more than other peoples, are given to laughing over their troubles. Few failed to appreciate the comic value of the fact that the "floating" of the peso was decreed on 23 March, which in Bolivia happens to be the official Day of the Sea.

CHAPTER 4

A SUMMING UP

Regression analysis of the Latin American data suggests that monetary growth explains the larger share of the observed cross-country variation in average annual inflation rates. Correlation does not necessarily imply causality, however, and it is often argued that the money supply is a passive variable that simply responds to inflation.

On the other hand, the analysis of monetary aggregates in Latin America shows that the tremendous monetary growth registered in this region is due to factors that, in principle, are controllable by the monetary authorities.[1] Over 90% of monetary growth is due to expansion in the monetary base, which involves a physical act of monetary creation that would seem to strain the notion of causality interpreted in such a "reverse" sense, and sometimes an additional share is due to changes in the money multiplier, which are partly due to changes in required reserve ratios. Thus, the greater share of monetary growth is due to factors that are or can be independent of the rate of inflation. This conclusion, taken jointly with the strong empirical correlation between monetary growth and price inflation, implies that the direction of causality runs from money to prices, and not the other way around, as it is often argued.

To be sure, the close correlation between monetary growth and price inflation has never been denied by structuralists, who argue, however, that such statistical correlations are irrelevant from the point of view of explaining the phenomenon. In part, this reflects to some extent a semantic disagreement as to what constitutes an explanation in the study of social phenomena, or, more precisely, a disagreement as to the meaning of the imputation of causality. Broadly speaking, "monetarists" tend to interpret the empirical relationship between money and prices as a causal relationship to the extent that: Increases in the money supply are invariably associated with price inflation, and significant price inflation never occurs in the absence of changes in the money supply.

The high empirical correlation between rates of price inflation and rates of monetary growth (adjusted for changes in real income) is thus taken as evidence in favor of this theory, which claims no more (and no less) than these twin statements. To monetarists, whose overall methodological approach is a statistical-econometric one, this constitutes in effect a sufficient causal explanation of the phenomenon of inflation.

To structuralists, however, whose approach is more attuned to "political economy" than to economics interpreted in a narrow, technical sense, this explanation is deemed insufficient, as it says nothing about the causal factors that underlie the observed monetary expansion. To monetarists this question is not meaningless, though it is one that is not amenable to analysis in strictly economic categories—a "meta-economic" question, as it were—since in principle the increase in the money supply can be due to any number of "ultimate causes." (Perhaps it would be better to speak of *reasons* rather than causes in this context.) The monetary view is thus a general theory of inflation, within the limits of its claim to generality. Beyond these limits the search for a general theory is a rather hopeless quest, since comparative analysis of inflationary episodes in different countries during specific historical periods yields a picture of such irreducible diversity that it virtually precludes the possibility of any general explanatory hypothesis.

Few adherents to the monetary view would quarrel, for instance, with one of the opening sentences in Sunkel's (1958) seminal paper: "The simple truth is that inflation does not occur *in vacuo*, but within a country's historical, social, political, and institutional framework." In a sense, that is precisely the point. It is hard to deny that, ultimately, specific inflationary episodes must be explained by reference to factors that transcend the purely formal, even mechanical relationships posited by the monetary approach, but such deeper explanations must of necessity refer to conditions prevailing in a specific historical time and place.[2]

Even a less than general theory, applicable only to the contemporary Latin American scene, seems to breakdown. In any case, we have seen that more often than not the empirical data are simply inconsistent with the predictions of the structuralist theories, which in practice raise more questions than they settle. The monetary history of individual Latin American countries is better explained by country-specific conditions than by the structural characteristics that these economies purportedly share in common. The Bolivian experience is a case in point.

The moral of the story is that, while the monetarist framework must underlie any explanation of inflation, the diversity of observed experiences rules out any general theory in the "deeper" sense. Ultimately, inflation cannot be fully understood unless it is viewed in historical perspective, the missing element in both the monetarist analysis, which is impersonal, as well as in the structuralist theory, which is deterministic. The historical approach to the explanation of inflation moreover highlights the human element, which the great monetarist-structuralist debate disregards altogether.

An inescapable conclusion of the study of monetary history, however, is the important and decisive role of personalities in the determination of economic trends.

This is clearly borne out by the Bolivian experience. Bolivian monetary history simply does not admit an interpretation analogous to the Tolstoyean view of military history: the notion that strategy and tactics do not actually matter a damn on the battlefield, where confusion reigns, the variables are infinite, and chance governs all. Quite the contrary. Time and again the action, frequently the *in*-action, of certain individuals has permanently altered the course of events. The previous runaway Bolivian inflation, that of the period 1952–56, was stopped in its tracks by the very same Dr. Siles Zuazo who presided over the most recent crisis. Indeed, the detailed account of the Stabilization Plan of 1957 by the U.S. economist George J. Eder (who designed the plan and was in many ways the eminence grise of Bolivian monetary policy at that time) clearly shows that the eventual stabilization of the peso was due solely to the decisive action of Dr. Siles, surmounting almost superhuman obstacles in one of the most critical political moments in recent Bolivian history.[3]

That was why is was believed, even by the opposition, that the accession to power of the "hero of '57" would again bring about a new stabilization. Unfortunately, if effective actions say anything about the ideas that guide them, we can only conclude that in the years between his two presidential terms Siles radically changed his mind on monetary policy, rejecting the monetary orthodoxy he so successfully applied in 1957, adopting instead the old Keynesian credo of salvation through public spending. (Bolivia is a land of contradictions, and the most recent inflationary crisis is rich in historical ironies, not the least of which the fact that Dr. Paz Estensoro is now attempting to stem the disaster he has inherited from Siles Zuazo, and to do so he is applying measures very much like those which Siles himself applied in 1957—to end the inflation that *he* inherited from Paz Estensoro, no less! To complete the historical cycle, the major opponent to Dr. Siles's stabilization program of 1957 was—who else?—Juan Lechín.)

Since we have cited in passing the theories of John Maynard Keynes, it seems appropriate to close with a quotation from the last page of his *General Theory*, which is highly relevant in this context:

> The ideas of economists and political philosophers, both when they are right and when they are wrong, are more powerful than is commonly understood. Indeed, the world is ruled by little else. Practical men, who believe themselves to be quite exempt from any intellectual influence, are usually the slaves of some defunct economist. Madmen in authority, who hear voices in the air, are distilling their frenzy from some academic scribbler of a few years back. I am sure that the power

of vested interests is vastly exaggerated compared with the gradual encroachment of ideas. Not, indeed, immediately, but after a certain interval; for in the field of economic and political philosophy there are not many who are influenced by new theories after they are twenty-five or thirty years of age, so that the ideas which civil servants and politicans and even agitators apply to current events are not likely to be the newest. But, soon or late, it is ideas, not vested interests which are dangerous for good or evil (1936, pp. 383–84).

The preceding quotation does not induce much optimism regarding the power of ideas in the short run (few economists would care to become "influential" if they must first become defunct economists!), but the personal experience of Lord Keynes, who was in fact highly influential even during his own lifetime, would seem to argue that he apparently underestimated the short-run impact of ideas on action. Keynes is also the author of another celebrated phrase, which has been the source of many misinterpretations that have caused much mischief in the recent past: "In the long run we are all dead." Unfortunately, problems will not just go away even if they are relegated to the limbo of the long run. The long run begins tomorrow.

NOTES

1. Recall, however, the comments in Note 6, Chapter 1. In the context of this discussion, the relevant question is whether the external sector component of the monetary base is responsive to the rate of domestic price inflation. To the extent that an increase in domestic prices can be expected to induce, ceteris paribus, a deterioration in the balance of payments, then inflation, will have, if anything, a negative impact on monetary growth.

2. Few inflationary episodes have been as closely scrutinized as the Chilean case, both from the structuralist viewpoint (see the references in Note 1, Chapter 2), as well as from the monetarist perspective—for example, Harberger (1963), and Deaver (1970). It is significant, therefore, that when explaining the repeated failure of attempts at monetary stabilization in Chile, authors of both camps ultimately and invariably resort to explanation in terms of that country's specific historical-political situation. The following passage in Sunkel's oft-cited paper is highly revealing in this regard: "This mechanism is fundamentally the result of Chilean society's political failure to resolve two great clashes of economic interests" (1958, p. 575). For detailed analyses of the political factors underlying the Chilean inflation up to around 1960 see Davis (1963), Grunwald (1961), and Schott (1959)—Grove (1951) is also relevant and informative. To be sure, it is frequently the case that passages from these texts can be applied (mutatis mutandis, but often verbatim) to the description of conditions prevailing in other inflationary economies, but this implies only that certain sociopolitical scenarios are (1) conducive to monetary inflation, and/or (2) militate against monetary

stabilization, and certainly cannot be elevated to the status of a general theory of the type envisioned by the original structuralist program.

3. See Eder (1968). Eder's account is briefly summarized in Yeager et al. (1981), pp. 108-19. Eder was not given to qualifying the expression of his personal judgments. In his book the ruling party in Bolivia during 1956 is described as "perhaps the most corrupt, incompetent and opportunistic group of politicians that had ever ruled the destinies of the nation" (p. 241). The importance of the human element in Bolivian monetary history is also well illustrated by another curious incident: from 1953 to 1956 the Bolivian government had been "advised" by a U.N. official, the Hungarian Arthur Karasz, and it may not be irrelevant that Karasz had been the president of his country' central bank during the Hungarian hyperinflation of 1945-46, which set the current world's record.

STATISTICAL ASPECTS OF INFLATION RATES

INTRODUCTION

Though there is a well-established body of knowledge concerning the fundamental determinants of long-run inflation (see Chapter 1), it is well known, on the other hand, that long-run relationships such as that of the Quantity Theory of Money fail to hold over short-run periods. Even so, perhaps owing to the explanatory power of theories of long-run movements, it is generally felt that the behavior of inflation in the short run is not fundamentally different from that of long-run inflation in terms of its basic determinants, and much work has consisted of attempts to extend the long-run theories to short-run contexts via, for instance, distributed lag equations and related techniques. To be sure, the validity of these approaches depends crucially upon the statistical properties of short-run inflation rates.

Apart from some recent studies of the variability of inflation rates (Logue and Willett, 1976; Foster, 1978; Holland, 1984; Ram, 1985) not much work has been done in this perhaps overly descriptive, preliminary field of the "statistical aspects" of inflation. This appendix, which analyzes the quarterly inflation rates of 15 Latin American countries over the period 1970–80, will hence address questions such as randomness, distributional form, and the behavior of extreme values.

RANDOMNESS IN INFLATION RATES

In the study of the time behavior of economic variables, an important question that arises is whether an observed increase (or decrease) in any given period will affect the likelihood of an increase (or decrease) in subsequent periods. In a random walk process, changes in successive periods are independent in a probability sense, and in any given period positive (+) and negative (−) changes are equally likely. Successive changes are then viewed as essentially random drawings from a symmetric probability density with zero mean.

To be sure, it is never possible to *prove* that a given empirical sequence has been generated randomly (Chaitin, 1975). On the other hand, the *hypothesis* of random generation can be tested statistically, and the series can be shown to be consistent (or not) with that hypothesis. A common test for randomness in this sense is based on the observed sequence of runs of positive and negative changes in the series. In a runs test, the observed number of unbroken runs of successive + and − changes is compared with the expected number of runs under the null hypothesis of independent and equally likely changes. A series that is rising or falling more or less smoothly will exhibit relatively long sequences of +s and −s, and hence a smaller number of runs than in an erratic series where + and − changes are distributed randomly.

Table A.1 shows the number of runs of + and − changes in the quarterly rates of inflation of 15 Latin American countries for the period March

Table A.1
Runs Analysis of Changes in Quarterly Inflation Rates

	Positive Changes	Negative Changes	Runs
Argentina	22	20	27
Bolivia	24	18	30
Brazil	21	21	29
Chile	21	21	23
Colombia	24	18	24
Dominican Republic	21	21	30
Ecuador	24	18	31
El Salvador	17	25	29
Guatemala	23	19	27
Honduras	18	24	32
Mexico	24	18	30
Paraguay	24	18	27
Peru	23	19	30
Uruguay	24	18	27
Venezuela	21	21	25
Totals, Average	331	299	28.1

Note: Expected Runs: 28.33
Standard Deviation: 2.71
5% Lower, Upper Limits: 23.0, 33.6

Source: Computed from data reported in *International Financial Statistics*, "Supplement on Price Statistics," Supplement Series No. 2, 1981.

1970–December 1980.[1] Following Moore (1968), the expected number of "runs up and down," d, in a randomly moving series is given by

$$E(d) = \frac{2n - 1}{3} = 28.33,$$

with variance $(16n - 29)/90 = 7.32$, where $n = 43$ is the number of observations in the original series. In no case is the observed number of runs significantly different from the expected number, and for the sample as a whole the average number of runs is practically equal to the theoretical expected value (likewise, the sample standard deviation, 2.63, is practically identical to the theoretical value of 2.71).

THE DISTRIBUTION OF CHANGES IN INFLATION RATES

Summary statistics for the Latin American data are shown in Table A.2. The mean changes in quarterly inflation rates are quite small, which is consistent with a random walk without "drift." (There is a tendency for the mean changes to be slightly positive, but whatever "drift" this may imply is practically swamped by the relative variability of inflation through time.) The variability of changes in inflation rates has been measured by the standard deviation of quarterly changes (s), and alternatively, following Foster (1978), by the mean absolute change $\overline{x}_a$. If successive changes are independent and normally distributed these sample statistics will be related by a factor of proportionality. In fact, the ratio of these statistics was proposed by Geary (1947) as a test of normality, and is hence often referred to as the "Geary ratio" (Kendall and Buckland, 1960). In the case of normal distributions $\overline{x}_a$ provides no additional information as its expectation is simply 0.8 σ, but if the distribution of changes in inflation rates is not normal, then $\overline{x}_a$ may well be a more relevant measure of variability. (Fama, 1963, has pointed out that in the more general class of stable Paretian distributions with characteristic exponent $\alpha > 1$, the mean deviation will have finite expectation even if the variance is infinite.)

The Geary ratios suggest strongly that the distribution of changes departs from normality, in some cases only mildly, in others more so. The average value of 0.72 is significantly less than 0.8 (on the basis of a conventional t-test based on the sample standard deviation of 0.07), and hence for the sample as a whole the normality assumption can be flatly rejected. A complementary test for normality is based on the "studentized range," that is, the difference between the largest and the smallest values in a sample, both expressed in standard deviation units. This statistic, which is highly dependent

Table A.2
Summary Statistics for Latin American Inflation, 1970–80

	Changes in Quarterly Inflation Rates (percent per quarter)						
	Mean Change	Standard Dev. (s)	Mean Abs. Change ($\bar{x}_a$)	Geary Ratio	Largest + Change	Largest − Change	Studentized Range
Argentina	0.34	14.11	9.73	0.69	45.29	−35.11	5.69
Bolivia	0.13	9.13	5.43	0.59	22.74	−28.81	5.65
Brazil	0.39	3.20	2.51	0.78	8.13	−5.83	4.36
Chile	0.04	16.21	9.71	0.60	49.94	−45.66	5.89
Colombia	0.04	3.72	2.66	0.71	5.34	−13.33	5.02
Dominican Rep.	0.06	4.56	3.41	0.75	9.55	−15.86	5.57
Ecuador	0.07	2.89	2.31	0.80	7.13	−6.41	4.68
El Salvador	0.02	3.16	2.47	0.78	6.89	−6.77	4.32
Guatemala	−0.11	5.29	3.82	0.72	12.50	−14.99	5.19
Honduras	0.005	5.06	4.24	0.84	11.31	−8.24	3.86
Mexico	0.12	2.48	1.80	0.73	7.89	−5.89	5.55
Paraguay	−0.02	5.98	3.94	0.66	18.13	−24.11	7.06
Peru	0.24	6.33	4.66	0.74	20.43	−17.49	5.99
Uruguay	0.06	8.25	6.14	0.74	18.40	−19.14	4.55
Venezuela	0.17	1.81	1.31	0.72	5.43	−4.62	5.55
Average	0.104			0.723			5.26
Std. Dev.	0.134			0.068			0.81

Source: Computed from data reported in *International Financial Statistics*, "Supplement on Price Statistics" Supplement Series No. 2, 1981.

on the extreme values in a sample, is appropriate for testing divergence from normality in the extreme areas of a distribution (that is, in testing for the presence of "fat tails"). In a normal distribution, the 5% upper critical value for the studentized range statistic is approximately 5.2 in a sample of 42 observations (by interpolation from the table reported in David et al., 1954, p. 491), which is exceeded in 9 out of the 15 cases. Overall, the distribution of changes in inflation rates seems to be characterized by slightly "fat tails," though there are some exceptions (which, not surprisingly, generally correspond to those cases where the Geary ratio is closest to 0.8).

The generally small value of the Geary ratio suggests a greater preponderance of small changes than under a normal distribution, while the studentized range suggests a greater frequency of extreme values. To adjust for differing variability, the observations were standardized in terms of standard deviation units, and the absolute values were classified in intervals of 0.5 standard deviations. The resulting empirical frequencies were then grouped for the entire sample of 15 countries, and compared with expected frequencies under a normal distribution (Table A.3). The results clearly show a departure from normality in the sense that there are "too many" small changes, "not enough" middle changes, and "too many" extreme values. This type of pattern is also known to characterize distributions of speculative prices such as common stocks—indeed, there is a strikingly close similarity between the distributions of changes in inflation rates and those of stock price changes (on the distribution of changes in stock prices see Fama, 1963, and Brealey, 1969, pp. 38–41). As Brealey notes in relation to the pattern of stock price changes, this is not meant to imply that divergence from normality involves some kind of deformity, though any theory of short-run inflation must account for this relative abundance of small changes, which would indicate a tendency toward persistence of inflation at given levels.

On the other hand, a striking feature of the time sequence of absolute changes is the inordinate degree of clustering of extreme values. Indeed, the distribution, by length, of runs of extreme values indicates that the departure from randomness is so strong as to suggest that repeated runs of extreme values do not really "belong" to the same distribution (Table A.4). This conclusion is buttressed by a closer inspection of these repeated runs. Of the 17 runs of length 2, for instance, 15 were of the form + − , a large increase followed by a decrease of about the same magnitude, and 2 were of the form − + . Hence these observations do not conform to the random walk model insofar as repeated runs of extreme values follow a pattern of reversal—these cases would appear to involve a kind of "catching-up" of the absolute price level, followed by a reversal to lower, more normal inflation rates.

Appendix

Table A.3
Distribution of Absolute Changes in Quarterly Inflation

Intervals in Std. Deviations	Proportion of Observations (%)		
	Normal	Observed	Stock Prices*
0.0 - 0.5	38.3	48.6	46.7
0.5 - 1.0	30.0	25.9	28.0
1.0 - 1.5	18.4	13.0	13.8
1.5 - 2.0	8.8	6.2	6.3
2.0 - 2.5	3.3	3.6	2.8
2.5 - 3.0	1.0	1.3	1.3
> 3.0	0.2	1.4	1.1

Note: As reported in Brealey (1969), p. 41

Source: Computed from data reported in *International Financial Statistics* "Supplement on Price Statistics" Supplement Series No. 2, 1981.

SUMMARY OF RESULTS AND SOME SUGGESTED HYPOTHESES

Any theory of short-run inflation must be consistent with the three main findings of the preceding analysis:

1. The proximate random walk behavior of inflation rates;
2. The relative preponderance of very small changes in inflation rates; and
3. The catching-up/reversal behavior of a large proportion of extreme values.

Random walks in prices of assets traded in specialized auction markets, such as common stocks, commodity futures, and foreign exchange, have been justified on grounds of market efficiency, as such prices can be expected to "fully reflect" all available information, and hence will only change upon the generation of new information, which is by definition unpredictable up to the moment it is generated (see Brealey, 1969, pp. 3–20, and Fama, 1970). It seems far-fetched, however, to invoke such an explanation for the random behavior of inflation rates, as it is generally agreed that short-run inflation, if anything, *fails* to fully keep up with movements in its basic long-run determinants, which has been the basic rationale for the application of distributed lags to the long-run relationships that are known to hold

Table A.4
Runs Distribution of Extreme Values

Runs of Length	Observed	Expected*
1	31	68.91
2	17	4.31
3	1	0.36
4	0	0.03
5	1	0.00
6	1	0.00
Average Run	1.55	1.07

Note: Extreme values defined (arbitrarily) as absolute changes greater than 1.5 standard deviations ($= 12.5\%$ of total sample). Expected frequencies of runs of length x given by the geometric density function:

$$f(x) = \frac{630}{x} \, 0.875(0.125)^x$$

Source: Computed from data reported in *International Financial Statistics*, "Supplement on Price Statistics" Supplement Series No. 2, 1981.

between inflation rates, monetary growth, and real economic growth. These approaches, however, are basically inconsistent with the random walk behavior of short-run inflation. For instance, the reduced form of a typical distributed lag equation derived from a partial adjustment process (see Nerlove, 1968) is of the form:

$$y_t = \alpha \beta x_t + (1 - \beta)y_{t-1} + u_t \qquad (0 \leqslant \beta \leqslant 1) \tag{A.1}$$

where y_t is the dependent variable, x_t an independent variable (or vector of independent variables), and β the "coefficient of adjustment." If y_t follows a random walk:

$$y_t = y_{t-1} + e_t \tag{A.2}$$

then a regression estimate of the coefficient of the lagged dependent variable, y_{t-1}, in equation (A.1) will be biased toward 1, indicating a very slow rate of adjustment per period. On the other hand, if (A.1) is expressed in the mathematically equivalent first-difference form:

$$y_t - y_{t-1} = \alpha \beta (x_t - x_{t-1}) + (1 - \beta)(y_{t-1} - y_{t-2}) + u_t - u_{t-1} \tag{A.3}$$

then regression estimates yield the opposite conclusion, since the estimated coefficient of the lagged dependent variable will be biased toward 0, indicating a more or less complete adjustment within one period. Thus, regression estimates of distributed lag equations involving random walks yield inconsistent results.[2]

The abnormal behavior of extreme values might be due to the effect of changes in expectations about the course of future inflation. As Kessel and Alchian (1962) have noted, for any given state of expectations there exists some current level of prices consistent with the desires of a community to hold wealth in different forms (monetary and real assets), and an increase in current expectations of future inflation, which implies a higher opportunity cost of holding monetary assets, will thereby induce a communitywide attempt to shift from monetary to real assets, a decline in the demand for money in real terms, and a corresponding rise in the price level associated with the fall in the real value of the money supply. If expectations had previously underestimated the course of inflation, the transition from unexpected to accurately anticipated inflation will produce a once and for all adjustment of this type in the price level, after which the rate of inflation should revert to lower levels, and should not accelerate in the absence of changes in underlying determinants. (On the other hand, the high probability of reversal of extreme values is in turn relevant for theories of the formation of inflationary expectations. The occurrence of extreme values induces a larger than normal degree of uncertainty as to future inflation, since it may be followed by a reversal to lower levels, or it may signal a transition to permanently higher levels. This situation can be expected to induce turbulence in prices of assets that are sensitive to changes in the rate of inflation, as a result of conflicting interpretations of the meaning of an inflationary signal. To use a phrase that denotes a recent trend in macroeconomic theory, one may well wonder what a "rational expectation" would be in this situation.)

Alternatively, this behavior may be accounted for by a process in which the persistence of inflation at given levels leads to an accumulation of inflationary pressures in excess of observed rates which in turn, once some critical tension is achieved, results in a sudden release, possibly in response to some triggering event.

It is not clear how these two interpretations might be distinguished empirically, and whether they are not in fact complementary. In any case, the relationship between short-run inflation and changes in long-run determinants is clearly a complex one, and methods that have served well for long-run hypotheses may be ill-suited for short-run contexts.

NOTES

1. Quarterly inflation defined as the percentage change in the Consumer Price Index from the last month of a given quarter to the last month of the following quarter. Hence there are 44 quarterly observations on the CPI, but only 43 quarterly inflation rates, and 42 changes in inflation rates. Data are from the uniform CPI series reported in *International Financial Statistics*, "Supplement on Price Statistics," Supplement Series No. 2, 1981.

2. Several pitfalls in the estimation of regression equations involving random walks are discussed by Granger and Newbold (1974), who do not, however, discuss the specific case of distributed lags.

BIBLIOGRAPHY

Agarwala, Ramgopal. Price Distortions and Growth in Developing Countries. World Bank Staff Working Papers No. 575. Washington: World Bank, 1983.

Aghevli, Bijan B., and Mohsin S. Khan. Government Deficits and the Inflationary Process in Developing Countries. *IMF Staff Papers* 25 (Sept 1978) 383–416.

Assael, Héctor, and A. Núñez del Prado. América Latina y la Inflación Importada, 1972–74. *El Trimestre Económico* 43 (Oct-Dec 1976) 969–1002.

Alexander, Robert J. Bolivia's Democratic Experiment. *Current History* 84 (Feb 1985): 73–76, 86–87.

Baer, Werner. The Inflation Controversy in Latin America: A Survey. *Latin American Research Review* 2 (Spring 1967) 3–25.

Baer, Werner and Isaac Kerstenetzky, eds. *Inflation and Growth in Latin America*. Homewood, Ill.: R. D. Irwin, 1964.

Balbach, Anatol B. How Controllable is Money Growth? *Federal Reserve Bank of St. Louis Review* 63 (April 1981) 3–12.

Baumol, William. The Transactions Demand for Cash: An Inventory-Theoretic Approach. *Quarterly Journal of Economics* 66 (Nov 1952) 545–56.

Boorman, John T. The Evidence on the Demand for Money: Theoretical Formulations and Empirical Results. In John T. Boorman and Thomas M. Havrilesky, eds., *Current Issues in Monetary Theory and Policy*, 2nd ed., 315–60. Arlington Heights, Ill.: AHM Publishing, 1980.

Brealey, R. A. *An Introduction to Risk and Return from Common Stock*. Cambridge: MIT Press, 1969.

Bronfenbrenner, Martin. Inflation and Deflation. *International Encyclopedia of the Social Sciences*, vol. 7, 289–301 (New York: Macmillan, 1968).

Bronfenbrenner, Martin and F. D. Holzman. Survey of Inflation Theory. *American Economic Review* 53 (Sept 1963) 593–661.

Cagan, Phillip. The Monetary Dynamics of Hyperinflation. In M. Friedman, ed., *Studies in the Quantity Theory of Money* 23–117. Chicago: Univ. of Chicago Press, 1956.

Campos, Roberto de Oliveira. Two Views on Inflation in Latin America. In A. O. Hirschman, ed., *Latin American Issues*, 69–79. New York: Twentieth Century Fund, 1961.

Canavese, Alfredo J. The Structuralist Explanation in the Theory of Inflation. *World Development* 10 (July 1982) 523–29.

Chaitin, G. J. Randomness and Mathematical Proof. *Scientific American* 232 (May 1975) 47–52.

Cole, Julio H. Inflation in Latin America, 1970–1980. *Government and Policy* 4 (Feb 1986) 31–41.

Cortázar, R., and J. Marshall. Indice de Precios al Consumidor en Chile, 1970–1978. *Colección Estudios CIEPLAN*, No. 4. Santiago de Chile, Nov 1980.

Crockett, A., and O. Evans. Demand for Money in Middle Eastern Countries. *IMF Staff Papers* 27 (Sept 1980) 543–77.

David, H. A., H. O. Hartley, and E. S. Pearson. The Distribution of the Ratio, in a Single Normal Sample, of Range to Standard Deviation. *Biometrika*, 41 (1954) 482–93.

Davis, Tom E. Eight Decades of Inflation in Chile, 1879–1959: A Political Interpretation. *Journal of Political Economy* 71 (Aug 1963) 389–97.

Deaver, John V. The Chilean Inflation and the Demand for Money. In D. Meiselman, ed., *Varieties of Monetary Experience*, 7–67. Chicago: Univ. of Chicago Press, 1970.

Dorrance, Graeme S. Inflation and Growth: The Statistical Evidence. *IMF Staff Papers* 13 (Mar 1966) 82–101.

Eder, George Jackson. *Inflation and Development in Latin America. A Case History of Inflation and Stabilization in Bolivia.* Ann Arbor: Univ. of Michigan, 1968.

Fama, Eugene F. Mandelbrot and the Stable Paretian Hypothesis. *Journal of Business* 36 (Oct 1963) 420–29.

———. Efficient Capital Markets: A Review of Theory and Empirical Work. *Journal of Finance* 25 (May 1970) 383–417.

———. Inflation, Output, and Money. *Journal of Business* 55 (April 1982) 201–31.

Feige, Edgar L., and Douglas K. Pearce. The Substitutability of Money and Near-Monies: A Survey of the Time-Series Evidence. *Journal of Economic Literature* 15 (June 1977) 439–69.

Ferrer, Aldo. El Monetarismo en Argentina y Chile. Part I, *Comercio Exterior* 31 (Jan 1981) 3–13. Part II, *Comercio Exterior* 31 (Feb 1981) 176–92.

Ffrench-Davis, Ricardo. The Monetarist Experiment in Chile: A Critical Survey. *World Development* 11 (Nov 1983) 905–26.

Fishlow, Albert. Indexing Brazilian Style: Inflation Without Tears? *Brookings Papers on Economic Activity*, No. 1 (1974) 261–82.

Fortín, Carlos. The Failure of Repressive Monetarism: Chile, 1973–83. *Third World Quarterly* 6 (April 1984) 310–26.

Foster, Edward. The Variability of Inflation. *Review of Economics and Statistics* 60 (Aug 1978) 346–50.

Friedman, Milton. The Quantity Theory of Money—A Restatement. In M. Friedman, ed., *Studies in the Quantity Theory of Money* 3–21. Chicago: Univ. of Chicago Press, 1956.

———. The Demand for Money: Some Theoretical and Empirical Results. *Journal of Political Economy* 67 (Aug 1959) 327–51.

———. Money: Quantity Theory. *International Encylopedia of the Social Sciences* vol. 10, 432–47 (New York: Macmillan, 1968).

———. *The Optimum Quantity of Money and Other Essays*. Chicago: Aldine, 1969.

Frisch, Helmut. Inflation Theory 1963–1975: A 'Second Generation' Survey. *Journal of Economic Literature* 15 (Dec 1977) 1,289–1,317.

Galbis, Vicente. Inflación: La Experiencia Latinoamericana, 1970–79. *Finanzas y Desarrollo* 19 (Sept 1982) 22–26.

Geary, R. C. Testing for Normality. *Biometrika* 34 (1947) 209–42.

Granger, C. W. J., and P. Newbold. Spurious Regressions in Econometrics. *Journal of Econometrics* 2 (1974) 111–20.

Griffin, Keith. *Subdesarrollo en Hispanoamérica.* Buenos Aires: Amorrortu, 1972.

Grove, David L. The Role of the Banking System in the Chilean Inflation. *IMF Staff Papers* 2 (Sept 1951) 33–59.

Grunwald, Joseph. The 'Structuralist' School on Price Stabilization and Economic Development: The Chilean Case. In A. O. Hirschman, ed., *Latin American Issues*, 95–123. New York: Twentieth Century Fund, 1961.

Gurley, John G., and Edward S. Shaw. *Money in a Theory of Finance.* Washington: Brookings Institution, 1960.

Guzmán Ferrer, Martín. Los Cuellos de Botella Inflacionarios en la Infra-estructura Económica. *Comercio Exterior* 24 (Jan 1974) 49–67.

Harberger, Arnold C. The Dynamics of Inflation in Chile. In C. F. Christ et al., *Measurement in Economics: Studies in Mathematical Economics and Econometrics in Memory of Yehuda Grunfeld*, 219–50. Stanford: Stanford Univ. Press, 1963.

Hazlitt, Henry. *Economics in One Lesson.* New York: MacFadden-Bartell, 1962.

Hirschman, A. O., ed. *Latin American Issues: Essays and Comments.* New York: Twentieth Century Fund, 1961.

Holland, A. S. Does Higher Inflation Lead to More Uncertain Inflation? *Federal Reserve Bank of St. Louis Review* 66 (Feb 1984) 15–26.

Johnson, O. E. G. On Growth and Inflation in Developing Countries. *IMF Staff Papers* 31 (Dec 1984) 636–60.

Judd, John P., and John L. Scadding. The Search for a Stable Money Demand Function: A Survey of the Post-1973 Literature. *Journal of Economic Literature* 20 (Sept 1982) 993–1,023.

Kafka, Alexandre. Indexing for Inflation in Brazil. In H. Giersch et al., *Essays on Inflation and Indexation*, 87–98. Washington: American Enterprise Institute, 1974.

Kendall, M. G., and W. R. Buckland. *A Dictionary of Statistical Terms*, 2nd ed. New York: Hafner, 1960.

Kessel, Reuben A., and Armen A. Alchian. Effects of Inflation. *Journal of Political Economy* 70 (Dec 1962) 521–37.

Keynes, John Maynard. *The General Theory of Employment Interest and Money.* London: Macmillan, 1936.

Klein, Herbert S. *Bolivia: The Evolution of a Multi-Ethnic Society.* New York: Oxford Univ. Press, 1982.

Klein, John J. German Money and Prices, 1932–44. In M. Friedman, ed., *Studies in the Quantity Theory of Money*, 119–59. Chicago: Univ. of Chicago Press, 1956.

Kravis, Irving B. Comparative Studies of National Incomes and Prices. *Journal of Economic Literature* 22 (Mar 1984) 1–39.

Ladman, J. L., ed. *Modern-Day Bolivia: Legacy of the Revolution and Prospects for the Future.* Tempe, Arizona: Arizona State University, 1982.

Logue, D. E., and T. D. Willett. A Note on the Relation Between the Rate and the Variability of Inflation. *Economica* 43 (May 1976) 151–58.

Martino, Antonio. Measuring Italy's Underground Economy. *Policy Review* 16 (Spring 1981) 87–106.

Meiselman, David. Worldwide Inflation: A Monetarist View. In D. Meiselman and A. Laffer, eds., *The Phenomenon of Worldwide Inflation*, 69–112. Washington: American Enterprise Institute, 1975.

Mitchell, C. The New Authoritarianism in Bolivia. *Current History* 80 (Feb 1981) 75–78, 89.

Moore, P. G. Non-Parametric Statistics: Runs. *International Encyclopedia of the Social Sciences* vol. 11, 190–96 (New York: Macmillan, 1968).

Morgenstern, Oskar. *On the Accuracy of Economic Observations*, 2nd ed. Princeton: Princeton Univ. Press, 1963.

Nerlove, Marc. Distributed Lags. *International Encyclopedia of the Social Sciences*, vol. 4, 214–17 (New York: Macmillan, 1968).

Officer, Lawrence H. The Purchasing-Power-Parity Theory of Exchange Rates: A Review Article. *IMF Staff Papers* 23 (Mar 1976) 1–60.

Olivera, J. H. G. La Teoría No-Monetaria de la Inflación. *El Trimestre Económico* 27 (Oct#Dec 1960) 616#28.

———. On Structural Inflation and Latin American Structuralism. *Oxford Economic Papers* 16 (Nov 1964) 321–32.

———. Money, Prices, and Fiscal Lags: A Note on the Dynamics of Inflation. *Banca Nazionale del Lavoro Quarterly Review* 20 (Sept 1967) 258–67..

———. A Note on Passive Money, Inflation, and Economic Growth. *Journal of Money, Credit and Banking* 3 (Feb 1971) 137–44.

———. Estanflación Estructural. *Desarrollo Económico* 77 (Apr–Jun 1980) 41–48.

Padvalskis-Simkus, Delia de. Review of O. Sunkel et al., *Inflación y Estructura Económica*. *Revista de la Integración* 1 (Nov 1967) 282–85.

Penrose, Edith. Money, Prices, and Economic Expansion in the Middle East, 1952–60. *Rivista Internazionale de Scienze Economiche e Commerciali*, 9 (May 1962) 401–27.

Pinto, Aníbal. Una Visión Latinoamericana de la Inflación en lose Paises Industrializados. *Comercio Exterior* 25 (Sept 1975) 1,023–33.

Prebisch, Raúl. Economic Development or Monetary Stability: The False Dilemma. *Economic Bulletin for Latin America* 6 (Mar 1961) 1–25.

Queiser Morales, W. Bolivia Moves Toward Democracy. *Current History* 78 (Feb 1980) 76–79, 86–88.

Ram, R. Level and Variability of Inflation: Time-Series and Cross-Section Evidence from 117 Countries. *Economica* 52 (May 1985) 209–23.

Rodríguez, Octavio. La Teoría del Subdesarrollo de la CEPAL: Síntesis y Crítica. *Comercio Exterior* 29 (Nov 1979) 1,177–93.

Schott, Francis H. Inflation and Stabilization Efforts in Chile, 1953–58. *Inter-American Economic Affairs* 13 (Winter 1959) 4–14.

Schultze, Charles. Recent Inflation in the United States. Study Paper No. 1, *Employment, Growth, and Price Levels*, 4–16. Washington: Joint Economic Committee, 1959.

Seers, Dudley. A Theory of Inflation and Growth in Under-Developed Countries

Based on the Experience of Latin America. *Oxford Economic Papers* 14 (June 1962) 173-95.

Sunkel, Osvaldo. La Inflación Chilena: Un Enfoque Heterodoxo. *El Trimestre Económico 25 (Oct#Dec 1958) 570#99.*

Sunkel, Osvaldo, et al., *Inflación y Estructura Económica.* Buenos Aires: Paidós, 1967.

Tobin, James. Liquidity Preference as Behavior Towards Risk. *Review of Economic Studies* 25 (Feb 1958) 65-86.

Tun Wai, U. The Relation Between Inflation and Economic Development: A Statistical Inductive Study. *IMF Staff Papers* 7 (Oct 1959) 307-17.

Vogel, Robert C. The Dynamics of Inflation in Latin America, 1950-1969. *American Economic Review* 64 (Mar 1974) 102-14.

Yeager, Leland, et al. *Experiences with Stopping Inflation.* Washington: American Enterprise Institute, 1981.

INDEX

Agarwala, Ramgopal, 29
Aghevli, Bijan B., 52
Alchian, Armen A., 78
Alexander, Robert J., 64
Aramayo, Carlos Víctor, 47
Argentina, 1, 21, 33
Assael, Hector, 37

Baer, W., 25, 36
Balbach, Anatol B., 23
Banzer, Hugo, 48, 60, 61, 63
Barrientos Ortuño, René, 48
Baumol, William, 4
Bolivia: balance of payments, 41–44,
    51; banking system, 56; exchange
    rate, 40, 50–51, 53–55, 61, 62, 64;
    external debt, 44–45; money supply,
    40, 55–56, 59, 62–63; public
    finance, 51–53, 56, 59; recent
    political history, 46–49; stabilization
    programs, 59–61, 67
Boorman, John T., 5
Brazil, 29–30, 33
Brealey, R. A., 75, 76
Bronfenbrenner, M., 36
Buckland, W. R., 73
Busch, German, 47

Cagan, Philip, 5, 39
Campos, Roberto de Oliveira, 25
Canavese, Alfredo J., 27
Chaco War (1932–35), 46–47
Chaitin, G., 72
Consumer Price Index (CPI), 8, 10–11,
    31, 58, 79
correlation vs. causality, 13, 65
Chile, 1, 6, 21, 68–69, 33

Colombia, 20
Costa Rica, 20, 32
Crockett, A., 6, 23

Davis, Tom E., 68
Deaver, John V., 68
distributed lags, 77–78
Dominican Republic, 12
Dorrance, Graeme S., 29

Ecuador, 20, 32
Eder, George Jackson, 67, 69
elasticity, defined, 22
elasticity, pessimism, 28
El Salvador, 20
Evans, O., 6, 23
expectations, inflationary, 5, 7, 13,
    23, 37, 51–52, 78

Fama, Eugene F., 21–22, 72, 75, 76
Feige, Edgar L., 5
Ferrer, Aldo, 36
Ffrench-Davis, Ricardo, 36
Fishlow, Albert, 30
food prices, in Latin America, 31–33
Fortin, Carlos, 36
Foster, Edward, 71, 73
Friedman, Milton, 2–3, 23
Frisch, H., 36

Galbis, Vicente, 33, 34
Garcia Meza, Luis, 49, 50
Geary, R. C., 73
Geary ratio, 73–75
Granger, C. W. J., 79
Griffin, Keith, 31
Gross Domestic Product (GDP)
    deflator, 8, 10

Grove, David L., 68
Grunwald, Joseph, 36, 68
Gueiler, Lidia, 50
Guevara, "Che", 48
Guevara Arce, Walter, 48, 49
Gurley, John G., 5
Guzman Ferrer, Martin, 27

Harberger, Arnold C., 6, 68
Hazlitt, Henry, 39
high-powered money, 14 (*see also* Monetary Base)
Hochschild, Mauricio, 47
Holland, A. S., 71
Holzman, F. D., 36
Honduras, 20
hyperinflation, 5, 7, 39

Import-Inflation hypothesis, 34–36
Inflation: and economic growth, 28–30; and relative prices, 29–30; and import prices, 33–36, 37; and public finance, 51–52; in Argentina, 1; in Bolivia, 1, 39–64; in Brazil, 29–30; in Chile, 1, 68; in Latin America, 1, 8, 11, 13–15, 71–79; in Uruguay, 1; monetarist theory, 6–7, 29, 65 (*see also* Quantity Theory of Money); non-monetary theory, 27–28, 37; structuralist theory (*see* Structuralist Theory of Inflation)
inflation rates: distribution of extreme values, 75; lack of normality in, 74–75; log-transformed, 7, 10, 13; randomness in, 71–73; short run vs. long run, 57, 71, 76; variability of, 71, 73–75
inflationary expectations (*see* expectations, inflationary)
International Monetary Fund (IMF), 36
Italy, money/income ratio in, 22

Johnson, O. E. G., 29
Judd, John P., 5

Kafka, Alexandre, 30
Karasz, Arthur, 69

Kendall, M. G., 73
Kerstenetzky, I., 25
Kessel, R. A., 78
Keynes, J. M., 4, 67–68
Kahn, Mohsin S., 52
Klein, Herbert S., 22, 64
Kravis, I. B., 23

Ladman, J. L., 64
Lechín, Juan, 47, 58, 61, 67
Liquidity trap, 4
Logue, D. E., 71

Martino, Antonio, 22
Meiselman, David, 10
Mexico, 17, 20
Mitchell, C., 64
Monetary Base, 14–16, 21, 23, 68; in Latin America, 17, 65
money: demand for, 2–3; determinants, 3–6; income-elasticity, 3–4, 6–7, 12, 22–23; inflationary expectations and, 5, 8, 13, 37, 78; interest rates and, 4–5; in underdeveloped countries, 6, 23
money/income ratio, 3, 22–23
Money Multiplier, 14–16; in Latin America, 17
Money, Quantity Theory of (*see* Quantity Theory of Money)
Money Supply: determinants, 14–16; in Latin America, 8, 10–11, 12, 14, 16–22; defined, 8, 14; real vs. nominal, 2–3
Moore, P. G., 73
Morgenstern, Oskar, 23

Natusch, Alberto, 49
Nerlove, Marc, 77
Newbold, P., 79
Nicaragua, 12
Núñez del Prado, A., 37

Officer, Lawrence H., 37
Olivera, J. H. G., 27–28, 36, 52
Ovando Candia, Alfredo, 48

Padilla, David, 49
Padvalskis-Simkus, Delia de, 36
Paraguay, 46
Patiño, Antenor, 47
Paz Estensoro, Victor, 47, 48, 54,
    60–61, 62, 67
Pearce, Douglas K., 5
Penrose, 22
Pereda Asbun, Juan, 49
Peru, 20, 33
Pinto, Anibal, 36
Prebisch, Raul, 36
purchasing power parity, 37

Quantity Theory of Money, 2, 6–7,
    8–10, 13, 21, 71
Queiser Morales, W., 64

Ram, R., 71
random walks, 72, 76–77, 79
required reserve ratios, 15, 18–21
reserves ratio, 18–21
Reserve Requirements (*see* required
    reserve ratios)
Rodriguez, Octavio, 36
runs test (for randomness), 72–73

savings ratio, 15, 18–21
Scadding, John L., 5
Schott, Francis H., 68
Schultze, Charles, 28
Seers, Dudley, 36
Shaw, Edward S., 5

Siles Salinas, Luis A., 48
Siles Zuazo, Hernan, 39, 47, 48, 49,
    52, 54, 58–60, 63, 67
Structuralist Theory of Inflation,
    25–37; and monetarist analysis, 25,
    27, 36, 65–67, 68; classification of
    inflationary pressures, 26–27; em-
    pirical evidence, 28–36; food prices
    in, 30–31; import bottleneck, 27,
    28, 33–36; major structuralist
    authors, 36; role of agriculture, 27,
    28, 37
studentized range test (for normality),
    74–75
Sunkel, Osvaldo, 25–27, 36, 37, 66, 68

Tobin, James, 5
Torrelio, Celso, 49, 50
Torres, Juan José, 48
Tun Wai, U, 29

Uruguay, 1, 31, 33
United States: demand for money in,
    4–5, 23; inflation in, 1

Venezuela, 20, 32
Vildoso, Guido, 49
Villaroel, Gualberto, 47
Vogel, Robert C., 6, 11–12

Willett, T. D., 71

Yeager, Leland, 69

ABOUT THE AUTHOR

JULIO HAROLD COLE was born in the Panama Canal Zone on June 5, 1955. After graduating from Universidad Francisco Marroquín in Guatemala (cum laude, 1978), he studied advanced courses in economics and statistics at the University of Rochester, New York. He has worked as a credit officer with the Bank of America NT & SA, Santa Cruz, Bolivia Branch, and was Administrative Manager of La Bélgica Sugar Mill, in Santa Cruz. He is currently Professor of Money and Banking at Universidad Francisco Marroquín, and has published several articles in the fields of inflation, development economics, and international trade. He is married and has one boy.